Justin

Merry Christ⟨mas⟩ ♡ **W9-AKN-497**

I know Lisa who
wrote this book and
believed you would
enjoy reading the book
since you spent good
times there with your
Grandpa John
Love, Grandma

P.S. Lisa has autographed this
book for you

The dragline that "walked" from Sunrise to Hope, and then made history.

I once asked Mom how anybody made love in a one-room cabin with three other people just the other side of a blanket "wall." "Very quietly," she said with a smile. "Very quietly." Well, quietly or not, that night was the start of the Dragline Kid. Everything worked just dandy, thank you.

Born in pre-World War II Seward, Alaska, gateway to the Kenai Peninsula; reared in a miner's cabin in the hamlet of Hope and then as the daughter of the postmistress in the burgeoning village of Kenai; an aspiring teenage model in 1950s Washington, D.C. ...

Lisa Augustine writes with disarming frankness about her early years, tales of hilarity and heartbreak, faith and determination. Her recollections are often earthy, sometimes opinionated, always lively. And along the way we learn how the Dragline Kid became Arlene Maxene Rheingans Hotchkiss Lisa Marie Graham Augustine.

Printed in the United States of America

First printed June 2002

Hardscratch Press, Walnut Creek, California

Library of Congress Control Number 2001099468

ISBN: 0-9678989-3-5

Cataloging-In-Publication Data

Augustine, Lisa.
 The dragline kid : a gold-miner's daughter from Hope, Alaska / by Lisa Augustine.

 p. cm.
 Includes bibliographical references and index.

 ISBN 0-9678989-3-5
  1. Augustine, Lisa. 2. Pioneers – Alaska – Kenai Peninsula – Biography.
 3. Frontier and pioneer life – Alaska – Kenai Peninsula. 4. Kenai Peninsula
 (Alaska) – Biography. 5. Kenai Peninsula (Alaska) – History.   I. Title.

F910.7.A93A93 2002
979.8/3—dc20   2002-099468

9 8 7 6 5 4 3 2 1

The Dragline Kid

A gold-miner's daughter from Hope, Alaska
[... finds adventure in Kenai, Alaska, but hits pay-dirt Outside]

By Lisa Augustine

For Justin — I hope my book will
bring happy memories of your visit to
Alaska via the Alcan hwy.
Lisa Augustine

Goldilocks and the Four Bears

WHEN I WAS A LITTLE GIRL in Hope, Alaska, I identified with Goldilocks. Bears were a common part of my childhood landscape, and because I had golden curls and a taste for porridge (which we called mush), I figured Goldilocks and I had a lot in common. However, I thought I had an edge on the little housebreaker. She had only three bears, whereas I had four.

Mom often spoke of my four bears, recounting favorite family stories and fleshing them out with fascinating personalities. It wasn't until she got out the worn black album and began putting faces to names and tales that I realized my "four bears" had only two legs and very little hair and were actually forebears. It was a disappointment, but as I grew I was eager to learn more about our Minnesota family, to better understand these distant kin and thus to feel a part of something bigger and more interesting than my little corner of the world.

A recitation of even my recent ancestral tree may not be of interest to anybody except my own descendants. It may, however, give some insight into my character to know a little about some of those characters. If you're not my descendant, you may want to skip the next few pages and get down to the good stuff. If, however, you want to dive into my gene pool, read on:

MY FATHER, ERVIN WILLIAM RHEINGANS, was born April 29, 1906, on a farm in Shible Township, Swift County, Minnesota. He was the third of nine children, the second son of three boys and six girls. Dad died August 23, 1972, and is buried in Memory Lawn Cemetery, Phoenix, Arizona.

Dad's parents were William F. Rheingans and Wilhelmina Dorothy Alvina Leusmann Rheingans. William was born February 25, 1875, in Oakwood Township, Wabasha County, Minnesota, and died August 7, 1938. He is buried in the Appleton, Minnesota, cemetery.

Wilhelmina, known to many as Aunt Winnie, was born July 25, 1882, in Wittengen, Hanover, Germany. She came with her parents and sister, Helen, to the United States in 1888. She died December 2, 1935, and is also buried in the Appleton cemetery.

William's parents were Peter Rheingans and Christine Saueressig. Peter, born October 11, 1841, in Rheinbollen, Rhenish Province, Germany, came to the United States at the age of six. He served with the Union forces during the Civil War, as a member of the famed Company F of the Ninth Regiment of Wisconsin Volunteers, and saw three years of active fighting. He was one of only 300 men in the regiment who survived the war, out of an original contingent of 1,400; the others died on the battlefield or in notorious Libby Prison. Peter died June 27, 1925, having survived not only the war but four wives, and is buried in the Appleton cemetery. He had 97 direct descendants at the time of his death. I was not yet around to be counted.

Christine Saueressig was Peter's first wife. Born in 1850 to Maria Margaret Konrad Saueressig and Mathias Saueressig, she bore Peter five children and passed away at age 28, in 1878. I have a braid of her thick auburn hair.

My father's mother, Wilhelmina, was the daughter of Carl F. Leusmann and Mary Dargel. Carl was born December 14, 1841, in Wittengen. As a young man he served in the German army and fought in the Seven Weeks' War. He came close to death when a mini-ball lodged in a knapsack he was wearing. I'm proud to have that mini-ball, and Great-Grandpa Carl's thimble. He later became a fireman and then a shoemaker. Carl married Mary Dargel on March 20, 1847, and immigrated to the United States 15 years later. He cobbled shoes until he saved passage money for Mary and their two daughters, Wilhelmina Alvina and Helen. Carl died June 6, 1928.

Mary Dargel was the illegitimate daughter of a titled German named von Knesbeck or von Konesenbeck and a young woman whose family name was Dargel. Mary's father was a voracious gambler who eventually lost everything at Monte Carlo – including his title, which he sold to pay his gambling debts. In addition to two daughters, Mary bore Carl a son who died as a young child in Germany. Mary died November 14, 1917.

I mentioned that Dad had eight brothers and sisters. They were: Rudolph, born 1901, died 1974; Lillian, born 1902, died 1976; Esther, born 1908, died 1983; Helen, born 1911, died 1991; Alvina, born 1914, died 1955; Alice (Leets), born 1915; Erlean, born 1917, died 1975; and Willard (Willy or Boydie), born 1923, died 1979.

Dad's family lived on the farm where most of them were born, until one by one they married and moved away.

MY MOTHER, JOYCE MARIE DORING RHEINGANS COOPER, was born January 6, 1911, in Sioux Falls, South Dakota. She was seventh in a family of nine children, five boys and four girls. She and my father were married November 27, 1930. Widowed in 1972, she married Richard A. Cooper on July 13, 1975. Richard died August 18, 1989. Mom passed away at age 90 on August 28, 2001, and is buried with Dad in Phoenix.

Mom's father, John Chester Doring, was born October 10, 1870, in Riverside, Wisconsin. He died in 1936 and is buried in Hutchinson, Minnesota. His family tree can be found in "The Ancestors and Descendants of Georg Werner Doring," compiled by my uncle, Donovan Doring, and his son, John Dale Doring, in 1991.

Mary Ruby Morris Doring, my mother's mother, was born October 12, 1878, in Viola, Illinois, and died in 1969. She too is buried in Hutchinson. She was the daughter of Edwin Morris, who was born in 1848 in Ohio and died in 1937, and Emma McFate Morris, born in Viola in 1857 and died in 1940. Edwin and Emma were married in 1877 and are buried in the Appleton, Minnesota, cemetery. Emma's father, another Civil War veteran, was Samuel Martin McFate, born in 1837 in Philadelphia, Pennsylvania, died April 8, 1900, in Viola.

Mom's siblings were: John, born in 1898, died 1950; Virginia, born 1900, died 1990; Edwin, born 1901, died 1925; Theodore, born in 1903, died 1981; Thelma, born 1905, died 1995; Adah, born 1907, died 1943; Donovan, born 1918, and Philip, born 1920.

Of the two sets of nine children, only Mom's two youngest brothers and Dad's sister Alice remain at this writing.

I WAS BORN AND REARED IN ALASKA. My parents' only child, I'm a native Alaskan, though not an Alaska Native. I am also, by virtue of having been born before 1958, a Territorian, or one who was born in a territory of the United States. This may not have been my biggest achievement, but it certainly has served me well as a conversation opener all my life. Beyond that, I'm sure my birthplace was responsible for many of my strengths, weaknesses, interests, and idiosyncrasies. Just as my ancestors must take some responsibility for my being me, so must my environment. A few years ago I wrote a poem that dealt with my folks' life in Alaska. Part of it, with apologies to Robert Service, goes:

> Alaska . . . a beautiful but frigid mistress:
> She would test you, she would take you
> She would bend you and would break you
> As she beckons with her tantalizing song.
> She would steal your dreams and haunt them
> 'Til you swear that you don't want them,
> Then she'd cast you out and back where you belong.
> . . .
>
> But oh, my friend, the glory,
> As you undertake the story
> That unfolds, and taste the challenge of each day.
> You will know when life is ended,
> Though you're broken, or you've bended,
> That you've lived a *life* somewhere along the way!

I am still fascinated by my forebears. In turn I hope my story will be of interest to future generations of our family. At the very least, this book explains how I came to be Arlene Maxene Rheingans Hotchkiss Lisa Marie Graham Augustine, a.k.a. the Dragline Kid.

In loving memory
of Joyce and Ervin Rheingans,
whose lives demonstrated faith, love,
courage and independence
to a grateful daughter

WITH hopes high this group of Salinas residents left the city last week for the Highland Creek gold mines, located near Hope, Alaska. Above, left to right, are Mr. Fred Mills, Mr. Louie Alves, Mr. Johnnie Silveira, Mr. Donald Warth, Mr. Lewis Tustin, Mrs. Joyce Rheingans and Mr. Irvin Rheingans. The party is making the trip by bus, boat, sled and caterpillar, and foot. At the mines, scene of the placer mining operations of the group, Mr. and Mrs. Leo Sears, and 3-months-old infant, Mr. Ray Sears and Mr. Charlie Mathison will join the party. Operations at the mine will start as soon as they arrive and will cease when the heavy snows arrive in October. Some will return to Salinas for the winter and others will move into Seward and Hope to while away the long northern nights. Mr. Tustin and Mr. Silveira are returning for their second season at the mines, as are the Sears and Mr. Mathison. The remainder, making their first trip, will be known as chechakos until they have raised beards—the men—that is.

untry

—Index-Journal, Post Engraving

Contents

The folks' house in Salinas

Hope

1

My folks began their life journey together in Minnesota in 1930. She was 19, he 24. Their wedding was at the beginning of a decade of disaster for our country, the era of the Great Depression. Both came from families of nine children and were the offspring of farmers. Their parents didn't have much of anything—except, apparently, healthy libidos—yet both my folks had happy childhoods.

They loved and respected their parents, and tolerated and were tolerated by their siblings, as well as can be expected in any family. Most of the time they loved those brothers and sisters, too. They had an abundance of other relatives and knew their neighbors on adjoining farms for miles around. Despite hard times, in later life they recalled mostly the good times, the times of laughter and warmth.

I suppose my father might have become a farmer, except that he wasn't the eldest son so didn't have much chance of inheritance. Farmland was beginning to dry up and blow away as the drought of the 1930s loomed, and Dad wanted to do his own thing, anyway. He had a dream. He wanted adventure. He'd been to California in his teens, had an aunt and uncle who lived out in Salinas, and he figured California was as close to the Promised Land as a fellow could get.

When he talked about California to Mom during their courtship years, it became *their* dream—an opportunity to forge a better life for themselves. Mom always liked nice things but had very little chance to obtain them. Most of the clothes she wore were hand-me-downs from three older sisters, all of whom had become schoolteachers. Mom was ready for a taste of "the good life."

In the '30s, a lot of farm folks with the same idea headed for California. Many of them had lost their farms, repossessed by banks when dust bowl conditions caused crop failures year after year. So it was "California or Bust!" My folks arrived before the main rush, so their situation wasn't quite as desperate as John Steinbeck's Joads, but it wasn't any picnic, either.

When they pulled into the Salinas Valley in their rickety International truck with a homemade wooden box that served as a tent frame on the back, they had to compete for the few available jobs with the "Okies" and "Arkies," terms that came to be used disparagingly for the Oklahomans and Arkansans who had already arrived (you have to wonder why there were no "Minnies").

It was easier in those days for women to find work than for men. Mom worked at various jobs: bean-sorter, housemaid, bakery counter girl, and cashier and bookkeeper in a meat market. Dad tried a number of schemes. He built a huge chicken house, but nary a chicken ever set foot in it—instead, he decided to raise pigeons to sell as specialty meat. Apparently, squab hadn't caught on with Californians yet, and the itinerant laborers couldn't afford the asking price, so that idea fizzled. But he planted a big vegetable garden, and flower patches, so with their squab they had a fairly well-balanced diet and a bit of decor to boot. It wasn't high living, but with Mom's wages it was survival. Eventually, Dad got a job as a mechanic in the ice plant where locally grown produce was kept cool before being shipped across the country.

My folks lived in Salinas for seven lean years, waiting for the seven fat years that never arrived. They drove home to Minnesota only once to visit their families, but that trip was well timed. The following year Dad's mother died, and the next year, Mom's father. A few years later, Dad's father passed away, also, so my folks never saw those loved ones again.

One day a woman came into the meat market where Mom worked, all a-gabble about her son, Louie Tustin, who had spent one summer gold-mining in Alaska and was heading back soon for another summer on the mine.

Over dinner that evening, Mom mentioned Louie and the gold mine to Dad. Eureka! There it was: The Dream, alive and well and living in a gold mine in Alaska.

The folks contacted young Louie and learned that although there were already several men and a cook involved in the venture, there was always room for one (or two) more—provided they had $700 to invest in the operation.

The plan was: Buy into the syndicate, work the mine all summer (the only season one *could* mine in that part of the world), find lots of gold, return to California in the fall, and enjoy the good life ever after.

That was the plan.

My folks scratched up the $700 and in March of 1937 set off by bus to Seattle with a bunch of young men from Salinas. On the bus Mom came down with chickenpox and was very nearly quarantined and forbidden to board the ship for Alaska. She talked the doctor into letting her sail, however, and after purchasing some north country clothes and other supplies, the group embarked on an Alaska Steamship Company vessel, the *Victoria.*

The voyage took five or six days, during which Mom kept hidden as much as possible while her poxes gradually faded. When the boat docked in Seward, on the eastern side of the Kenai Peninsula, the group loaded their gear and themselves aboard the train and rode to Moose Pass, about 40 miles northwest. There they piled their supplies onto a huge sled pulled by a Caterpillar tractor, owned by another miner they had met aboard ship, and headed over the snow-covered pass to Hope, a tiny town located where Resurrection Creek empties into Turnagain Arm. Their mine was near Hope. The very name was reassuring.

A few miles out of Moose Pass, Mom began to feel dizzy. It was time to stop for a "potty break," anyway, but since there were no potties around she waded through the deep snow into the trees for privacy. She had just pulled her ski pants back up when she passed out. The men eventually missed her, went seeking, and carried her back to the sled where she came to, despite or because of their pounding her on the back and trying to get her to down a shot of whiskey.

Fortunately, they soon realized what had caused the dizziness: The wind was blowing exhaust fumes from the "Cat" up around the sled and into Mom's face as she rode. After that she ran alongside the rig or rode the runners of the sled, taking turns with the men, until they arrived at a cabin on Summit Lake where they planned to spend the night. Oscar Dahl, who owned a hotel in Seward as well, had given them permission to use his cabin, and they bedded down on the floor.

After a quick breakfast the next morning, they covered only about 10 miles before the rig tipped over and spilled all their provisions into the snow. With the sled once again upright and reloaded they trudged on to Sunrise, an almost-ghost town where a couple named Johnson provided hospitality for the second night.

From there the eager miners pressed on to Hope, population approximately 75 assorted souls. It was afternoon and growing dark when they arrived and began looking for a place to overnight. Some of the boys bunked with locals, but my folks found a tiny abandoned cabin. The door was stuck partway open and snow had drifted in piles on the dirt floor. There was a decrepit potbellied stove for heat, and dried spruce boughs on a narrow bunk served for a mattress. The bunk was too narrow for two grown people to lie flat, so they crawled into their sleeping bags, still wearing their clothes, and curled up around each other like a couple of Malamute huskies.

Mom told me that before falling into an exhausted sleep she thought, "What in the world am I getting into? I must have rocks in my head!" Followed by a defiant, "So what? We're together, and we're setting off on a wonderful adventure—maybe with a pot of gold at the end."

The next morning the little group hiked a rough five miles into the mountains above Hope, to the mine and camp on Resurrection Creek, climbing over tailing piles left behind by earlier, turn-of-the-century miners. Someone with a truck transported their supplies three miles to the end of the "road," but from there they backpacked everything to the camp. It was April first, the birthday of one of the Salinas boys, Don Warth, so lots of kidding about the April Fool's boy made the going easier. A shaggy old dog named Rusty tagged along for company.

The mining camp contained the basics: a cookhouse, a bunkhouse for the guys, and a rough, unfinished cabin measuring 10 x 10 feet that was to serve as my parents' new home. On the raw board floor were a small heating stove, a few wooden kerosene boxes piled on top of each other for storage, and a full-size bed. Spikes in the wall served for hanging clothes.

That evening Mom was informed, "Oh, we forgot to tell you, Joyce. Our cook won't be up here until our first 'cleanup,' so I guess you're the cook." She'd never cooked for more than the two of them, and that announcement came as quite a shock. But she pitched in and did her best.

A couple named Jerry and Leo Sears and their baby lived about half a mile from the main camp, and Charlie Mathison and his wife, Ann, lived in another cabin at the camp. Ann was disabled, and Charlie did their cooking.

Joyce and Erv Rheingans, outside their cabin at the mine

Jerry Sears baked bread for the whole crew, and Charlie taught Mom how to make sourdough hotcakes from a starter that she kept alive by feeding it with flour and water each time she used the batter. She learned to make "syrup" from brown sugar and water. The miners started every morning with tall stacks of hotcakes, which kept them going until lunchtime, when canned meat sandwiches and coffee filled their growling stomachs. Those who didn't drink coffee made do with good, cold creek water.

Their initial supplies included potatoes, noodles, onions, hams, bacon, eggs, canned Spam and a variety of canned vegetables and fruits. Eventually the meat supply ran low, and although moose season was long past, it was decided to send someone out to kill some fresh meat.

Don Warth tried first. By then the spring grass and underbrush were high, and they soon lost sight of Don, a short young man, as he trudged away in his rain gear and hip boots. Even without the extra clothing, the going would have been tough. Fallen trees and thick thatches of tall "stinkweed," skunk cabbage and prickly devil's club made for slow progress.

The day grew darker and colder and there was no sign of Don. No one got much sleep that night. The next morning he finally showed up, in a lot of pain. He'd spent the night under a spruce tree where porcupines had once sheltered. As he lay unsuspecting on the quills, several worked through his clothes and into his back. Porcupine quills are barbed like fishhooks and must be removed, or they can work their way right through a person. Not a happy thought, especially since one harpoon-like quill was positioned directly behind Don's heart.

But who would do the surgery? Knives and razor blades were the only instruments at hand. One of the Sears brothers, Ray, a tall, strong fellow, volunteered as surgeon. He made one tiny cut with the razor blade and then fainted. Unfortunately, Don remained conscious. Nobody else wanted to take up the operation, so Don set out on his own for the hospital in Seward. He made his way down the creek to Hope and from there hiked the old wagon trail to Moose Pass, a two-day trek. Luckily, he caught the Anchorage train to Seward the afternoon he arrived in Moose Pass.

A week or so later Don returned and proudly showed off the site of his surgery, a crater about the size of a child's fist. He told Mom he'd stayed with the Sears brothers' parents while recuperating, but she later read an account in which he was quoted as saying that he was ministered to by women in the red light district who gave him aspirin and sleeping pills.

Meanwhile, of course, the meat situation remained critical. My dad went hunting next. He was an excellent shot, having had lots of practice in Minnesota, and I think he was very hungry. Conditions on the mountain were still miserable. Again it grew dark, and no Erv. Mom finally went to bed, but not to sleep. Around midnight the cabin door flew open and Dad fell exhausted face-down on the floor. Clutched in his fist was his big red bandanna, and spilling from the bandanna were the heart and liver of a moose.

The next morning liver and onions accompanied the hotcakes, and when all had eaten their fill, half a dozen of "the guys"—including one gal, my intrepid mother—helped haul the moosemeat back to camp. The going was worse than she could ever have imagined. Undergrowth was thick and high, and windfall trees were so long one couldn't go around them. She was humiliated when she had to have a boost to climb over the worst ones. And in her heavy, wet clothes, she was thoroughly miserable.

That moose dressed out at about 600 pounds and was a welcome change of diet. When they had eaten about half of the meat, a friend from Hope hastened up the mountain to report that the game warden, following an anonymous tip, was headed their way. Mom had a moose roast in the oven, so she whisked it over to Charlie's cabin and hid the rest of the fresh meat in big kerosene cans which the boys sank in the creek.

She quickly stuck the last ham in the oven, and when the warden arrived, he joined in a hearty ham lunch. He searched the camp, shrugged, said he must have been misinformed, and away he went. Mom doubted that he was fooled. He could see how low their food supply was, and being a good, kind man, he turned a blind eye. Moosemeat was to be a staple of our diet as long as we lived in Alaska. I think Dad killed a moose for every year of the 25 they lived there—most taken in season, however.

In the evenings the boys took turns cutting each other's hair as needed. About a mile farther up Resurrection Creek lived an old hermit named Carl Magnuson. On his way into Hope one day he stopped at their camp and asked if he could get a haircut. He was none too

Erv and Joyce Rheingans and the catch of the day

clean, but some of the boys offered, and then Mom offered. He wouldn't settle for them, however. He pointed to Dad and said majestically, "He will cut my hair." Dad had never cut even a dog's hair and tried in vain to get out of it. Mr. Magnuson insisted, and Dad chose to cooperate rather than rile him up. It was a butcher job, but the old fellow went away happy.

He continued down the mountain to Hope, but before long, his big white husky, Snowball, came tearing back and remained at the mine with my folks, who later learned that Mr. Magnuson had arrived in Hope completely insane. He ranted and raved and peeked into windows and generally gave the Hope folks a bad scare. He was escorted out to Morningside Hospital, a mental institution near Portland, Oregon. The boys teased that it was Dad's haircut that finally drove Mr. Magnuson over the edge. He never returned, so Dad adopted Snowball. Later, that dog went to Bob DeFrance to pay an important bill.

The miners had a "cleanup" in late June. They took the gold from the riffle box and proceeded to tally what all their hard work had accomplished. With pulses pounding, they gathered down at the creek. Peering through the water into the riffle box they could see the gold, shining like—well, like pure gold. A lot of pure gold. But as the water was let out, its magnifying power went with it. Then the gold didn't look so impressive. In fact, when it was assayed and sold, they had a grand total of $750 for three months' work to divide among them. Every bit of that money was spent to buy more food. The cook never did show up, so Mom had a permanent job. Louie Tustin, a cheerful young fellow, had broken his leg and was hobbling around on crutches and unable to mine. He became her helper.

Toward fall, salmon began coming up the creek to spawn. The miners were more than ready for a change of diet, and one late afternoon Dad disappeared and then reappeared to announce that he'd gaffed two big salmon. Delighted, the fellows went out to inspect the catch of the day. Soon they were back, asking where Dad had hidden the fish. There wasn't a fin or a scale to be found anywhere.

Old Rusty the dog looked a bit sly, but he wasn't talking. Finally someone spotted a mound of dead leaves. Underneath were the two salmon, hidden not quite well enough, and not by Dad. Washed off, cleaned and fried, the fish were consumed by the crew with great enjoyment, as Rusty wistfully looked on. Mom thought Rusty had been getting even with Dad, who had made a harness and backpack for the dog and enlisted Rusty to accompany him down the trail from time to time to haul back canned goods for the camp. Whenever Rusty saw Dad get out the harness, he'd run and hide.

After the June cleanup, the crew had set up the mining operation again and returned to the backbreaking job of separating the gold from its hiding place. They figured that since they knew what they were doing now, when cleanup came again the first of September, they should have a good haul. It was starting to freeze at night, and soon they would be unable to mine the creek anymore, so this was their last chance for a bonanza.

But they were disappointed again. This time they took in about $800. It was time to go home. When they divvied up, there was just enough money for the California boys to get passage home, though a couple of them stowed away aboard the ship in Seward. The men who lived in Hope year-round took their money and hiked into town. My folks found themselves with only $100 between them for the entire summer's work—not enough to leave and not enough to live the winter on. They were up the creek, financially as well as geographically. They decided to go north to Anchorage and find work to tide them through the winter.

But there was no work to be had in Anchorage. The Great Depression was just as depressing in Alaska, especially in the winter months. They were discouraged and desperate after almost a month of job-hunting when they ran into Charlie Mathison and his brother, Bob, in town buying supplies for their winter trapline. When these sympathetic fellows saw my folks' plight, they made an offer that couldn't be refused:

If Mom and Dad came with them on the trapline and helped run it, and if Mom continued providing her delicious meals and helped with Charlie's invalid wife, Ann, the Mathisons would split the fur money, giving the folks a third of the take. From that, the folks would pay the Mathisons for whatever food they ate during the months they would spend on the Chickaloon flats. They jumped at the chance.

Charlie was a funny little guy. He talked a lot, very fast, chomping on gum and compulsively wiping the tips of his fingers on the front of his shirt. He was the only person I've ever met who kept a

Erv and Joyce Rheingans with Erv's first Alaskan beaver pelt

Ann and Charlie Mathison and Erv Rheingans, at the Chickaloon cabin

gum board. On this homely piece of wood he arranged his wads of gum, re-chewing them in a sequence known only to himself.

Bob was taller, and thin, with a shock of straight dark hair falling over his forehead. He was a poet and a musician—played the violin. He was also a boatman. He built a scow and piloted it back and forth across Turnagain Arm to Anchorage, weather and tides permitting and depending on the necessity.

The Mathisons were somehow related to the Clark family, people you'll meet in the following pages. The Mathisons had arrived in Hope from Texas in the late 1800s, mined the creek and apparently had some good strikes. Their little mother had four children, three boys and a daughter who was lame and had to be carried. Besides being quite lucky at mining, the Mathisons' father owned and operated a prosperous sawmill on Bear Creek.

So Bob and Charlie were true Alaskan pioneers, and among the founding families of Hope. They were well versed in the ways of mining, trapping, hunting, and surviving, and my parents learned a lot from them.

For eight months, those five—Charlie, Ann, Bob, and my parents—lived together in a tiny cabin on the Chickaloon River about 10 miles from Hope, without electricity, indoor plumbing, telephones, stores, medical facilities, or ever seeing another human being. At times my folks "ran the line" alone, sleeping on spruce boughs under a canvas tent. Keep in mind that we're not talking about camping in Yellowstone Park in July. We're talking about Southcentral Alaska in the winter, where the temperature can drop to 20 and 30 degrees below zero.

Early one frosty morning Bob woke Dad, saying, "There's a moose down by the river and in range of your '30 aught 6.' Go get him, Erv." Dad jumped up and ran out of the cabin, wearing only his long johns and shoepacs. He took careful aim, and there was their meat for the winter. They dressed it and hung it in the woodshed where it froze almost immediately and provided a handy butcher shop whenever they needed a steak, ground meat, stew meat or roast. Of course the liver and heart went first; they were everybody's favorites.

The cold weather was good for trapping. Pelts were thick, and the beaver, otter, mink, muskrats, coyotes and ermine were plentiful. The following spring, in Anchorage, they sold the pelts to Mr. Green, a furrier, and after settling up with the Mathisons, my folks even had a little money left over.

They didn't have any prospects for the summer season, though. The boys from California weren't coming back, so that association was kaput. Charlie had plans to mine a different location on Resurrection Creek, only about three miles up from Hope. He invited Dad to join him and a few other local fellows.

Hope, Alaska, from near Carl and Emma Clark's place—
Rheingans' cabin is far lower left

2

THE FOLKS STILL DIDN'T HAVE a place to live, but since the Mathisons had proved to be agreeable hosts as well as employers-after-a-fashion, it was decided that my parents would share the Mathisons' Hope cabin with them. Dad hung a blanket across one end of the cabin, to form the folks' "room," and the five of them settled down for the summer.

In the late 1930s only about 75 people lived in the little village at the mouth of Resurrection Creek. Nestled among mountains on three sides, with tide flats on the fourth, Hope is at the northernmost part of the Kenai Peninsula and was originally a settlement of Athabaskan Indians. I don't know if the Russians ever stopped in Hope during their settlement of Alaska, but in 1888 a man named Alexander King rowed an old dory up Turnagain Arm from Kenai and months later showed up in Anchorage with a respectable amount of gold in his jeans. He claimed he worked $50 a day out of Resurrection Creek, and that boast was good enough to spark a lot of interest in the area.

Soon other prospectors arrived, and by 1894 they were mining not only on Resurrection but on nearby Bear Creek as well. The following spring, hordes of prospectors arrived, booking passage from the States to the eventual site of Seward, on Resurrection Bay, and hotfooting it across the peninsula toward what was to become Hope. At Six-Mile Creek they founded a town named Sunrise that eventually grew to some 1,000-plus souls, but many continued on to the Hope area. Would-be millionaires also arrived by sailing from the States to Cook Inlet and up Turnagain Arm. The youngest of the prospectors arriving on a ship called *Utopia* was named Percy Hope, and because of his youthful enthusiasm, the settlement that grew at the mouth of Resurrection Creek was named after him.

A number of those turn-of-the-century miners were still in Hope when we lived there, tough, weathered, furry-faced old "sourdoughs," still hoping. They came from varied, sometimes checkered pasts, these oldtimers, some hiding from families, unwanted wives and/or the law, some craving adventure, others just wanting to be left alone. But with

The infamous dragline in operation

very few exceptions, they were sweet, generous old gents. Some you'll meet later in my story.

The summer of 1938, Dad mined with Charlie Mathison, Joe Richards, George Brandell, a fellow nicknamed Frenchie Mallot, and Ken Hinchey, who many years later became the mayor of Anchorage. Joe was married to a Native woman named Alexander, and they had an adopted son, Georgie. Alexander got to be cook this time. Mom said she had a way of preparing porcupine that was so delicious you'd swear you were eating roast suckling pig.

Ken Hinchey's wife, Nadine, and Mom became good friends, often walking up to the mine with picnic lunches, and working together to separate the fine gold dust from sand and waste on cleanup days, after the nuggets had been removed. This process was tedious, but sometimes rewarding. After Joe Richards cleaned up most of the gold from the dark sand, he'd dump the dregs into a coffee can and give it to the women. At the kitchen table, they'd pour a small amount of the sandy gold onto white butcher paper. Then, taking a dried grass straw from the yard, they'd gently blow away the sand. The heavier gold dust would remain, gleaming against the white paper. There never was very much, but what there was was exciting.

Mining got a bit easier after Dad and some of the other men went over to the ghost town that had been Sunrise and "borrowed" an abandoned dragline. Webster defines a dragline as "an excavating machine having a bucket that is dropped from a boom and dragged toward the machine by a cable." I would further describe it as a huge piece of heavy equipment, similar to a steam shovel, which miners used to drag dirt and boulders and gravel out of the creek in search of the ever-elusive nugget.

This particular dragline was rusting away there in old Sunrise. So Dad and his buddies "walked" this monster about 14 miles to their own operation, cutting wood as they went and burning it to fuel the boiler and make steam with which to power the machine. They hauled water in barrels on a Model A pickup truck, from whatever creek, river or lake was handy along the route. Thus, creeping slowly along, the dragline "walked" to its new location in eight days. And then the real work began.

Ken Hinchey described the process in a booklet distributed by the Hope Centennial program committee in 1994:

Before we could start mining, a trench had to be
hand-dug. Then a 500-foot, 14-inch pipeline was laid—
reduced to 12 inches, and then to 8-inch line to feed the
sluice box. In "miner talk," this means that much water
was needed to wash the gold-bearing gravel (rocks and
sand), through the 30-inch by 40-foot sluice box with its
24-inch side walls. Railroad rails laid across the box were
the "riffles" designed to catch the raw gold. The rocks
and gravel—with plenty of water—would slide and roll
on top of the crossways rail-bars. It sometimes took two
men to coax the heaviest boulders on down the sluice;
damned hard work!

It was really hard work, prying the riffles out from the
box, since they were cemented in with heavy and
hardened "Bootlegger Cove" clay. But when loose, the
riffles could then be scraped and washed to allow all the
gold flakes and nuggets to fall into the final box. . . .
Soon, after the first three or four feet of the headbox was
unriffled and the sand and silt was water washed—the
gold swept into our "dust pan." Then it was dumped
into a sourdough gold pan where the experts took over.
We fellows pried, scraped, washed and scooped with our
dust pan—hoping to see more than what was usually
"skinny," but we told ourselves we knew it would be.

Then it was Joe Richards' turn—and then Mom and Nadine chose
their straws and finished "cleaning up" by collecting the most minute
specks of gold dust.

And so the summer of 1938 wound down. Days were getting
shorter again, nights colder. Soon the mining season would be over for
another year, and the little bit of gold in the Mason jar wasn't much to
brag about. (Ken Hinchey writes that they took about $6,000 worth
of gold that season. I think he exaggerates. If, however, he's correct,
my folks got precious little of it.)

One crisp morning, Dad went out to start the dragline. The
engine was cold and sluggish, and the crank of the flywheel didn't
want to turn over. As usual, Dad used his foot to turn the crank, which
was similar to that used on a Model A auto. Apparently he had set

32

Ken and Nadine Hinchey and Alexander Richards, right, at the mine

Pipeline to the mining site

the magneto timing too fast. That morning, when he kicked the crank, it spun around and kicked back. It lifted all 6'1" and 195 pounds of Erv Rheingans right up to the metal roof of the cab and knocked him out cold. As his body came crashing down, his legs apart, he straddled a narrow plank, crushing his testicles in the process. He then fell out of the cab and into the pit, on his head. Dragline – 1; Erv Rheingans – 0.

When the other fellows found him, he was still unconscious, and upon examining him they were horrified to see the state his "privates" were in. Young Georgie Richards ran the three miles down the creek to town to get Mom.

You can imagine her thoughts as she drove a borrowed old Ford coupe pell-mell up the trail, not knowing how badly her husband was injured—if he was even alive—and frantically wondering how in the world they would get him the necessary medical attention.

When she got to the mine, the fellows told her Erv would have to get to a doctor fast. But the closest doctor was in Seward, 75 miles away. Everyone agreed that the trip would probably kill him, so they simply loaded Dad into the little coupe and told Mom to do the best she could with him.

That summer Mom had become acquainted with the young wife of a longtime Hope resident named Carl Clark. Emma was a registered nurse, so on the way back to the Mathison cabin, Mom stopped and picked her up. With the help of young Georgie, they carried Dad into the cabin, undressed him, and got the shock of their lives. His penis and testicles were terribly swollen and rapidly turning black. Emma said they were filled with blood. Fortunately, she had some morphine on hand for emergencies, and they figured this more than qualified. When Dad finally came around, he was in horrible pain. The morphine helped somewhat, and the women began putting alternate hot and cold compresses on his injuries. For two days and two nights they kept the compresses going, and gradually "things" began to improve.

It was several weeks before Dad was even able to walk, and by then the mining season was over. Again their share wasn't enough to get them back to California. Even if it had been, Dad had lost all interest in California and was talking about making Alaska their home. Mom was less than thrilled, to put it mildly, but she was more worried about getting her husband back on his feet than whether they'd be spending the winter in sunny California or frigid Alaska.

In time Dad did recover. One night, after they crept beneath their shared sleeping bag, he whispered, "Maybe we'd better see if everything still works."

I once asked Mom how anybody made love in a one-room cabin with three other people just the other side of a blanket "wall." "Very quietly," she said with a smile. "Very quietly."

Well, quietly or not, that night was the start of the Dragline Kid. Everything worked just dandy, thank you.

3

By now my folks had been married almost eight years. During the California sojourn, they felt they were too broke to start a family and took precautions to avoid doing so. However, for several years Mom had been thinking that if they waited until they could afford one, they'd never have one. Before Dad's accident, even with the Mathisons virtually in their bedroom, they'd been trying. When month after month went by with no pregnancy, Mom had begun to worry. It seemed very unusual for a couple coming from such prolific families to have trouble conceiving. Inconceivable!

Her concern grew. Tests at the Seward Hospital showed both of them OK. She had her Fallopian tubes "blown" but that proved ineffective. She took hormone shots. Nothing. Next came various old wives' remedies, which included drinking gallons of beet juice and taking Lydia Pinkham's little pills, the label of which promised "A Baby In Every Bottle." There weren't any babies in her bottles, so she began to pray.

Be careful what you pray for, the saying goes. You might get it. Mom never dreamed it would take a round-house punch from a dragline to shake things up and get 'em going, but that's the way it happened.

When she missed her first period, she figured she'd "caught a cold in her bottom." This interesting ailment apparently wasn't uncommon in those days, though for some reason you never hear about it any more. (She often warned me not to sit in the snow, or on the ice, lest I catch a cold in my bottom, and I guess I was just real lucky.) Before Dad's accident, however, Mom had been up to the mine and had happened to sit on the ice-cold pipeline, so her self-diagnosis didn't seem far-fetched.

Presently she began having terrific bouts of nausea, especially in the morning. She thought she must have gotten the flu, or that she had a "complication to the cold in the bottom," and she kept on praying for a baby as she lost her breakfast each day.

Charlie

Charlie and Ann Mathison's cabin, where the Dragline Kid was conceived

M-105 Seward, Alaska

Seward hospital, late 1930s

After a few weeks of the nausea, she caught a ride to the doctor in Seward and was amazed and delighted to learn that she was, as they say, with child.

I don't think Dad was as thrilled as she was, but he got used to the idea. He didn't, however, care for the doctor's comment that if they ever wanted more children, Joyce would just have to give Erv a "good kick in the balls"—the doctor's expression. It may be no coincidence that I am an only child.

Everything continued to make Mom upchuck, especially the smell of bacon cooking. From September 'til Thanksgiving, she wasn't able to eat a decent meal. Which may account for the fact that I myself have never met a food I didn't like.

Now that their family was expanding, my folks thought they should have a place of their own. From Winfield Taylor, an Englishman who had given up on mining and moved away, they bought a cabin across the road from the store. The sale was handled by Elwyn Swetmann, the Seward druggist, who also dabbled in real estate. The price was $500, according to Mom, although I grew up thinking it was only $200. Well, she was there, and I wasn't (only minimally), so we'll have to take her word for it.

Winfield Taylor was apparently quite a poet. He left behind what looked to be several rough drafts of his work on a high shelf in the cabin. I think he could have given Robert Service a run for his money, and I've often wondered whatever became of him. One particular poem I found so extraordinary that I memorized it when I was about 12 and include it here for your edification:

DISAPPOINTMENT
By Winfield Taylor

Far out on a stream where the winters are quiet
And placer claims stretch in a limitless span,
Where porcupines rustle their pick handle diet
And otherwise mangle the labors of man,
A trapper abides in this land of tradition
And patiently toils for the fur he may glean,
Whose motive in life is a burning ambition
To capture a bunch of the shy Wolverine.
But try as he would, all his efforts were futile.

No matter how likely the spot he'd select,
Hard luck or the fates seemed derisive or brutal,
For the trap and the track always failed to connect.
At length, through much toil and profound meditation
A scheme was evolved that the vacancy filled.
"'Twill kitch erray critter that rambles creation,"
Thus musing, the trapper proceeded to build.
The frame was erected, all spots that had rusted
Were polished with care, and the levers were bent.
The parts all assembled were oiled and adjusted
And set to a hair with an evil intent.
Next morning he rose from a much disturbed slumber
By dreams of embracing the animal's form.
"I'll hustle," he said, "for I sure have his number,
And take off the pelt while the carcass is warm."
Approaching the spot of his crafty selection,
Imagine his wrath when he found he was stung.
For Wolverine tracks from most every direction
Surrounded the trap that had never been sprung.
Though the language ensuing defies demonstration,
The air turning blue from its virulent flow,
Profanity ceased when his keen observation
Discovered this scrawl in the beautiful snow:
"Dear Trapper," it read, "You will pardon my choosing
This sliver of willow in lieu of a pen.
The fact is, the fountain and tab I've been using
Were left on the pillow 'way back in my den.
Your latest invention I've just been appraising –
I haven't a doubt it's as clever as sin.
Though its strange mechanism is truly amazing
I'd likely get out, could I ever get in.
I have no intention of casting reflections
Upon a contrivance so skillfully wrought
But since you've omitted to furnish directions
There isn't much show for a guy to get caught.
This hellish machine of an evil conception,
Designed with the murderous motive to kill,
I leave for a creature of keener perception

To perish in proof of your marvelous skill.
Though sweet are the fumes of the baits you are wasting,
Your wiliest move I may read at a glance.
Far sweeter to me is my liberty tasting,
So cheese it, Oldtimer, there isn't a chance.
While some of your schemes are so slyly potential,
Your methods and lures of the finest I've seen,
My clothing in winter is highly essential.

      Respectfully yours,
      A Darn Cute Wolverine"

My dad said that captured the wolverine personality to a T.

The poet's weathered gray one-room log cabin had a rough wood floor. It came "completely furnished" with a bed, a small wooden table, several chairs, and two wood-burning stoves, one for cooking, the other for heating. There was no running water or indoor toilet, but Resurrection Creek flowed briskly about 250 feet from the back door, and we also had a well and an outhouse that stood between the cabin and the creek.

During the dark hours (and winters in Alaska are dark nearly the clock around), light was provided by kerosene lamps, which required frequent filling, washing and wick-trimming. As a family abode it made a pretty good miner's shanty, but the folks were happy to have some privacy at last, and a warm, snug place to call home.

Actually, it proved to be not all that snug. Spaces between the logs were chinked with moss and something that resembled plaster of Paris. Because the cabin was so old this mixture was dried and cracked, and pieces often fell out or were blown out during a particularly brisk williwaw. And later, little fingers would poke and pick until chunks crumbled and fell to the floor, creating a tiny slit-window from which to peer out at Hope's main street.

During the long winter of 1938, there still was no work to be had. Hope settled down to a dark, cold nap. The men occupied themselves with hunting and cutting firewood. The women "kept house," baked, did fancywork, and made clothes. And everybody did a lot of visiting back and forth. Newcomers, like my folks, had much to learn about living on the Last Frontier, so they appreciated any tips the oldtimers had to offer. Pete Sorenson was a favorite; hours flew by as he spun tales of his adventures. Other sourdoughs—Jimmy Newman, George Adney (who, it turned out, shared an Aunt Gussie Woolworth with my mom, so was a shirt-tail cousin), Cal Dryer, Hub Clark (Emma's father-in-law), Ed Haun, Al Ferrin, George Roll, the Buzard brothers, Mr. Carson (who was the town postmaster and had no legs), Tom Sobol and Sam Gates—all had wisdom to impart to eager and naive cheechako ears.

Cheechakos, in case you aren't familiar with the word, are folks who are new to Alaska.

Another poem I learned in my youth explains:

> When you've lived up in Alaska where the Arctic breezes
> blow,
> And have seen the fall ice coming and have seen the
> spring ice go,
> And survived one long, hard winter when the mercury
> ran low,
> You can drop the name "Cheechako"—you've become a
> "Sourdough"!

Technically, my folks weren't cheechakos anymore, having survived that miserable year on both the mine and the trapline, but they didn't feel like bona fide sourdoughs yet, either. They still had a lot to learn—and the tall tales made for fascinating entertainment on long winter evenings.

Ken and Nadine Hinchey returned to Anchorage, so Mom spent a lot of time with Emma Clark and Elizabeth Brenner, an older woman who had a family of grown boys and a pretty teen-age daughter. Mrs. Brenner taught Mom to knit, and Mom kept busy making a layette for "the baby." Emma was a big help during the pregnancy. Having a nurse across the road was a comfort and an education.

Alice Mitchell (whose husband, Roy, had a steel plate in his head from the war and was boss of the two-man crew that kept the road open between Hope and Moose Pass) threw a baby shower, and relatives in Minnesota sent a big box of tiny goodies. This child would be well clad.

In the early spring of 1939, Dad's kid brother, Willy, arrived. Both his parents had passed away, and he was lonesome for his big

Three seasons in Hope: The Clarks' house can be seen on the hill behind the Rheingans' cabin, top photo; in the center photo, Doc Nearhouse's store, left, is across the main street from the Rheingans' cabin, second from right; below, the small cabin between the Rheingans' place and their shed was built for young Willy Rheingans and years later housed the Hope library.

brother. Willy was only 16, and eager for the Alaska experience. He and Dad built a tiny log cabin across the path from the privy. They cut trees, skinned the logs and dragged them onto the site with whatever vehicle they could borrow. The snug cabin became Willy's place, and he settled in. That little cabin still stands on the same spot, having survived earthquakes, floods and some 56 winters. At one time it served as the Hope library building, though I heard recently that it has been sold.

Having a teen-age boy around was sometimes challenging, but usually it was a joy. Willy didn't like sitting on the frost-covered toilet bench, so he got hold of some sheepskin and lined the hole. You've heard of a fur-lined pot before? Well, we had a fur-lined privy seat. It made a unique statement, contrasting nicely with the Sears and "Monkey Ward" catalogues that were the only "bathroom tissue" we had at the time.

Willy's teenage complexion became a source of embarrassment to him. All available acne remedies failing, in desperation he decided to try some green liniment he'd found somewhere. This stuff burned the living daylights out of his tender face. Round and round the cabin he tore, yelling like a banshee, with a very pregnant Joyce right behind him, trying to get him to stop long enough for her to bathe his face. He eventually wound up at the creek, plunging his head repeatedly into the frigid, soothing water.

Another eventful day Emma came panting across the street yelling, "Your house is on fire!" Sure enough, the chimney pipe had overheated and caused a fire on the roof. With Willy's help, the women formed a bucket brigade and quickly doused the flames.

There were a number of young fellows around Hope that winter; the Brenner boys and the Hatch kids were Willy's good pals along with a young man with the last name of DeVine, who was soon dubbed "Father Devine." On Hallowe'en, the boys caught "Father Devine" in his outhouse, locked the door from the outside and tipped the privy over on its front. It was tricky business trying to crawl through the hole in the seat without falling into the pit.

The long winter passed, and finally it was spring. "The baby" was due on June first, and Mom didn't want to risk being late getting to the hospital in Seward. Here's what author-trucker Dennie McCart wrote in his book *The Hope Truckline and 75 Miles of Women*:

One day [during the third week of May, 1939] I got a
quick request to take Mrs. Joyce Rheingans to the
Seward hospital. She was expecting and was getting
warnings. We took off in the truck on rough roads with
seventy-five miles to go. Whoo-ee! Everything went all
right until we got over to Jerome Lake and the baby-to-
be must have started to complain as Joyce asked me to
stop. She got out and walked around some, but in about
five minutes she felt OK. Thank Gosh! as I sure didn't
want a baby to be born along the road with me as mid-
husband instead of an experienced mid-wife. Anyway, we
made it to Seward OK. She was happy to have that long
ride over with and I was very glad we had made the trip
without too much happening. It was almost two weeks
later when a nice baby girl was born.

Thank you, Dennie! We all got lucky that time.

Dennie dropped Mom off in Seward with the Searses, who lived
near the hospital. My parents had mined with two of the Searses' sons
the first season.

Poor Mom developed uremic poisoning. Her limbs and eyes were
puffed and waterlogged. The doctor decided to induce labor via injec-
tion. She stayed in the hospital all day and got several shots, but nothing happened. Thoroughly disgusted, she trudged back to the Sears
place and the next day appeared at the hospital hoping for better luck.
This time the doctor thought maybe a few good doses of castor oil
might help. That cleaned her out but didn't budge the baby one iota.
By June first, Mom was really miserable, but she waddled down to
Resurrection Bay and sat on a log to watch the boats and seagulls.
Suddenly she felt a dampness running down her legs into her shoes
and realized her water had broken.

Back to the Searses' she hastened, dripping all the way. When
Mrs. Sears called the hospital, the nurse said, "Now we're getting
somewhere. Come right over." At this writing, only a dusty empty lot
stands to mark the site of my nativity. But in 1939, the "new" Seward
Hospital was a mere nine years old and consisted of a basement, one
floor with approximately 25 double rooms including the nursery, and
an upper floor with offices and staff lounges. Mom was put in a room

with Helen DeFrance, the wife of another Hope miner, who had just given birth to a baby girl who was given the beautiful name Ramona. But Ramona was nicknamed Fuzzy, and as far as I know she is called Fuzzy to this day.

While Mom's travail was progressing (or not), Dad was working his tail off at the mine. He couldn't be spared to sit around a hospital waiting for a baby who apparently had no desire to face the world. It wasn't until Bob DeFrance picked up Helen and Fuzzy and took them home to Hope that Dad learned that his wife was in labor. He hitched the next possible ride to Seward, arriving June fourth, with plenty of time to spare.

Mom's labor pains, which had started June first, progressed in frequency and intensity until they came every five minutes on June third. She was exhausted. The doctor gave her a shot to help her sleep, with the unfortunate consequence that the baby "went back up." By now everyone was getting tired and just a little cranky. On the fourth, "the plug" dropped out, and it appeared that the baby was at last ready to make an appearance.

Dr. Ray Bannister, the man who had seen Mom through her pregnancy, and in whom she had great faith, had developed an infection in his hand and was unable to deliver the child. Instead, another doctor—who, according to disquieting rumor, had a strong yen for the strong stuff—took on the task. He stayed at the hospital all night on the fourth, occasionally peering in at Mom, who agonized in the delivery room, pushing and panting and pulling on Dad's necktie, while instruments bubbled merrily in a nearby sterilizer.

It's hard to tell who was more miserable: Mom had a five-day labor going, and Dad, who had been working practically around the clock, was being strangled by his own wife. He gave out before she did (but then, he had a choice, didn't he?) and finally staggered out to the doctors' lounge for a few minutes' rest and a gasp or two of air.

Through it all, Mom was determined not to yell. During her endless labor she'd heard another mother screaming, and she vowed she wouldn't embarrass herself like that. She didn't remember wishing for her own mother, either, for she had made up her mind that this was something she was just going to have to do all by herself. While she was pushing and grunting, she heard the doctor say grimly, "When Miss Murrell comes, we'll take that baby!"

Miss Murrell was an institution around the Seward hospital, a legend in her own time and ever since. She was a maiden lady of few words, but they were pithy words. When the celebrated Miss Murrell arrived, she ordered Mom, "Go ahead and scream. We've heard it before." But Mom just grunted and pushed, maintaining her chosen dignity.

Around 8 a.m. on June fifth, they gave her a shot to knock her out. With Miss Murrell's help, the doctor did a bit of snipping and then reached in with "high instruments" and, grasping me by the head, wrestled me into the world at 9:37.

The Dragline Kid had arrived.

Erv and Arlene Rheingans, 1939

4

Mom remembered pulling and pushing and hearing herself moan, and at last she heard Miss Murrell say, "It's a girl. She has the longest fingers I've ever seen." The next thing Mom knew, she was back in her room, waking up to see Dad looking weary and worried as he sat beside her bed. They asked to see me, but Miss Murrell said, "Nope, not for several days you don't want to see her. She looks like she came through the war." The doctor later admitted that he should have performed a Caesarean section, but he couldn't do that once he had induced labor with a shot.

My folks knew they couldn't intimidate Miss Murrell, so they just waited and worried and wondered what kind of little freak they'd produced. The following day Dad couldn't take the suspense any longer —besides which, he had to get back to the mine. He never said how he convinced Miss Murrell to exhibit me, but ta-dah . . . (drum roll, please) . . . suddenly there I was in all my many-colored splendor.

My right eye was swollen shut, with a purple shiner that would have made John L. Sullivan proud. A raw, red gash running through my eyelid and eyebrow, and another at the top back of my head, marked the spots where the forceps had grasped my tender skull. Miss Murrell was right: I was a mess. But Mom always maintained that my left eye—bright and blue as a jaybird, she said—was wide open, peering around with great interest and undeniable intelligence. She thought I was the prettiest thing she'd ever seen. Truly, there's no accounting for mother-love. There's no record of my dad's first impression of the fruit of his loins.

Dad had to get back to work, but Mom and I stayed in the hospital for 17 days, until our battle scars healed. Only one other woman came in to deliver her baby during that time. Marge Merkowski had a very short labor, delivered little Tony with a minimum of fuss and feathers, and left the hospital a couple of days later. Mom didn't mind her long convalescence, as she was thoroughly exhausted and extremely stiff and sore, and had to be bathed and turned regularly. I suspect she enjoyed the rest, and I know she enjoyed Miss Murrell's company.

I, on the other hand, wasn't happy. Mom could hear me crying in the nursery, even right after feeding time when I should have been full and content. This went on for a couple of weeks, until someone finally noticed that I wasn't gaining weight. It was determined that Mom's milk didn't have enough nutritive value, so I was given an additional formula, and from then on I never had one single bit of trouble gaining weight. Darn!

When word got back to Dad that we were ready to leave the hospital, and that the bill for our stay was $20, he found himself "a bit short." He didn't have any way to get us back to Hope and he didn't have $20. You may recall that Dad had acquired a beautiful white dog named Snowball whose former owner was taken to the insane asylum. Bob DeFrance was very fond of sled dogs and cast a covetous eye on Snowball, so Dad sold Snowball to him for $20. I was, you might say, bartered for a lunatic's dog.

Dad borrowed Bob Mathison's old Model T, and our little family returned home to Hope. The folks stopped at the mine first, to introduce me to Dad's partners. I'd been named Arlene Maxene Rheingans, but because of Dad's accident, to the miners I was the Dragline Kid.

The way I got my true name was this: I was born on June fifth, the birthday of Mom's younger brother, Donovan (called Donnie or Dono), and also the birthday of Dad's younger sister, Erlean. (If you're interested in numerology, you might find some significance in the fact that there were nine children in Mom's family, and nine children in Dad's family; Dad was the third from the eldest, Mom the third from the youngest. And I was born on my paternal aunt's *and* my maternal uncle's birthdays. Well, it always seemed significant to me.)

Anyway, Mom wanted to name me Donna, after Uncle Donnie. But Dad won the toss, and his sister was honored instead. Since Mom didn't care for the name Erlean, they compromised on Arlene. Maxene was the name of a friend who worked with Mom in the bakery in Salinas, and they thought the two names had a sort of pleasant rhythm. From the time I became aware of it I never approved of their choice.

This might be a good time to give you a more complete description of my parents. Mom was 5'5" tall, solidly built, with brown hair

Joyce and Erv Rheingans on the Chickaloon flats—
Erv took the picture using a string to trip the shutter

and blue eyes. She was an attractive woman, 28 years old when I was born. But I believe she became prettier as she grew older, not reaching her peak until she was in her 50s and 60s. She was one of the best-looking octogenarians I've ever seen. Even at 90, although she had lost an inch or two of height, she was slimmer than she'd ever been, and still had excellent posture. She was elected Rose Queen at her assisted living facility one year. Mom always loved pretty clothes, and even during those times when money was scarce she managed to dress well. She loved to sing and was a good conversationalist. However, she suffered from rather low self-esteem all her life, thinking herself not as attractive or thin or smart as she'd like to be, and probably as a consequence had a history of migraine headaches.

I think Mom's best quality, and greatest curse, was her eternal good nature. Physically she was strong, but she would rather switch than fight, preferring peace at any price. Consequently, she was a joy to be around, never complaining, never arguing, never insisting on her own way. Another trait that contributed to the headaches, I'm afraid.

Although Mom always had a sweet, gentle nature, she was a good disciplinarian. She used the "spank stick" when necessary, but instilled in me such respect and love that I never wanted to hurt or disappoint her, although, as you will see, I sometimes did. She tried to make me feel that I was the prettiest, the smartest, the cleverest, the most interesting child around. Since there were only about a dozen kids in all of Hope, the competition wasn't too tough, and I always knew she was prejudiced in my favor so didn't take her pride in me too seriously. She is, however, responsible for my own healthy self-esteem, a wonderful gift that proved to be a lifesaver years later when it was sorely needed.

Mom's deep religious faith enabled her to accept whatever came her way as "working together for good," and this made her brave as well as strong. A very outgoing person, she felt the lack of family and friends in Alaska, and I became not only her doll but her great joy and her friend. From Mom I inherited a love of singing, a good sense of humor, an even disposition, bass fiddle hips and little else. I could not have asked for a better mother.

Dad was 33 when I was born. He was 6 foot 1 and of medium build, also with blue eyes. As a young man, he had lots of thick, wavy brown hair, but to his consternation the hair started to go when he was in his mid-20s. I can only remember him with a receding hairline, which inched backward gradually for the rest of his life. He also had a slightly receding chin, but overall he was quite a nice-looking man.

From him I inherited my height, the shape of my hands, and the biggest ears since Dumbo. I've been told often that I look just like my dad.

As a child, Dad was rather sickly and was pampered by his mother. His birth was unusual in that he was one of a pair of twins whose twin was born dead some time before Dad arrived. I wonder if that could account for his solitary, introverted personality. At any rate, he too had rather low self-esteem. Although he was a good baseball player, an excellent mechanic (having attended mechanics school in St. Louis as a young man), a crack shot, and extremely clever at inventing and building, he never felt he had anything going for himself. Whereas Mom graduated from high school, he never did, and I think that bothered him, too.

He was a very quiet man. Could go for days without speaking, especially if he was annoyed about something. He preferred his own company and thoroughly enjoyed the life of trapping, fishing, hunting and other typically Alaskan pursuits.

My dad didn't smoke, drink, gamble or cuss. He didn't think one should even use derivatives of swear words, such as darn, or gosh. He never looked at another woman after he met my mother. His only vices, that I know of, were chewing snoose and a predisposition toward selfishness. He'd chewed since he was nine or 10. And he just quietly did whatever he wanted, without consulting or considering Mom or me. So he sometimes hurt us, not overtly, but by his lack of attention and companionship.

He was a good man. A complex man. But not the "Father Knows Best" kind of dad. Whether or not he realized it, he kept me from becoming self-centered and spoiled. The most memorable advice he ever gave me was: "Don't make a spectacle of yourself." He couldn't abide vanity or arrogance, so he kept me fairly humble. After I was five or six, he seemed to lose interest in me. While Mom made me feel like a little princess, he left me feeling somewhat uninteresting and unnecessary. Maybe we just made him feel left out. He never disciplined me, but I always feared that he might, and one silent, stern look from those steely blue eyes made me snap to attention. I never sassed or talked back to my dad, but always tried hard to please him or make him laugh. Occasionally, he'd crack a tiny crooked smile, and I knew I'd achieved a rare and wonderful thing.

I love my parents very much, and consider myself lucky indeed to have been born into their lives.

When we arrived at the little cabin in Hope, Willy was beside himself with excitement. He'd scrubbed the cabin until it fairly shone, using powdered lye on the wooden floors to bleach them snow white. In his passion for germ extermination he burned his hands quite badly, but he was so pleased with his efforts, and his new niece, that he hardly noticed.

After my exciting entrance into the world, summer in Hope progressed as usual, which is to say it was dedicated to mining and preparing for the following winter. Dad was working about three miles up the creek with Charlie Mathison and Joe Richards, at a different location than either of the two previous years. They came back to town late every evening, and got up in the wee morning hours to get an early start. This left a lot of time for Mom to play with her new doll.

At first she was scared spitless. Having had Miss Murrell and the other nurses to fetch and carry for her, she found herself suddenly and solely responsible for the care and feeding of a very small, noisy person. Most of it she learned to handle, but she was terrified of giving me a bath.

She'd been faithfully lathering me with baby oil several times a day, but due to her reluctance to give me a bath I developed a rank odor. She conceded that the inevitable could be put off no longer. First she stoked up the wood stoves to a red-hot roar so that Precious wouldn't catch cold. Then, sweating like a porker, she undressed me. But when she looked at my naked, slippery, rancid little body, she lost her nerve and prevailed upon Emma to give her a few lessons.

Some explanation: Bathing in those days was a complicated, once-a-week, only-if-you-really-need-to affair. Mom would hasten to tell you that she was religious about daily "spit baths," consisting of a wet soapy washrag applied to the more personal bits and pieces of the body. But I'm talking here about real baths.

Until I was a teenager, we bathed in a round, galvanized tin washtub. In the summer, this was filled by buckets from either the creek or

Willy Rheingans and his dog team at Hope

the well, and in the winter, with endless bucketloads of melted snow. The tub was placed on the kitchen stove to heat. By evening (always on Saturday), the water was warm enough, and the tub was first set up on the kitchen table where the water remained warmer; everyone knows heat rises, and our floors were always cold. First I would climb aboard for my bath. When I was scrubbed and toweled to within an inch of my life, Dad would lower the tub onto the floor so Mom could climb in. Finally, my tall, fish-belly-white-skinned dad had his turn. By then the water was cold, gray and scummy, but bathing last goes with being the dad.

My first bath wasn't quite that complicated. Instead of the big round washtub, the much smaller metal dishpan served as my bathtub. Once Mom got the hang of it, she kept me clean and shiny as a new penny.

Since I was her sole entertainment, she eventually drove me to distraction with her attentions: primping, scrubbing, curling, brushing, dressing up, dressing down, licking the hanky and wiping the dirty little face at every opportunity. Only because she got such a kick out of it was I able to tolerate her ablutions, and I believe she would have continued cleansing me ad infinitum if I hadn't finally gotten big enough to outrun her.

During that period, a Methodist minister drove over from Seward every few weeks to hold services. When I was a few months old, my folks thought I should be baptized, and so I was. Young Uncle Willy acted as godfather, and the indispensable Emma Clark was my godmother.

Willy was crazy about me, Mom said. Called me "Koooookie," and didn't feel a bit self-conscious pushing me around town in my baby buggy. The other fellows teased him, but he didn't give a fig. About that time I acquired yet another nickname. Dad called me "Pug" (pronounced "Poog") because of my short nose. Later he just called me the Kid, and he was still doing so when he passed away 30-some years later.

Emma Clark and Carla Mae, left, with Joyce Rheingans and Arlene, right; the mother and child in the middle aren't named in Joyce's old album.

5

I'M NOT SURE WHAT I ACTUALLY remember about my first four or five years. I recall a few incidents, and I heard so often about others that they seem like my own, personal remembrances. But I recollect distinctly the feeling of peace, security and simplicity that prevailed in our cabin and in the little village called Hope. Although the United States (and thus her territory, Alaska) was entering the Second World War, to a small child it seemed far away and of no consequence.

Uncle Willy abandoned us in April of 1940. He got homesick for the rest of his family back in Minnesota, and off he went. It wasn't long before we heard that he was in the Army, along with Uncles Donnie and Phil, and other young Americans.

That summer Dad mined for a month, this time with Uncle Earl Clark, a little lower down on Resurrection Creek. Again Mom was asked to cook for the men, so she and I spent the month going back and forth from town to the mine. Although I learned to walk at nine months, I was still wobbly on my feet, so Mom more than had her hands full keeping me and the rustic cook shack clean. She didn't mind the cooking, but she was happy to get back to her own antiseptic little cabin again.

Sometime during my first couple of years, an oldtimer named Jimmy Newman brought us two beautiful white Arctic fox neckscarves, one for Mom and one for me. They had been cured and made up by a professional furrier, and still had their legs, feet and heads attached. With beady black artificial eyes and silvery clasps that hooked them together, they were fit to bedeck Mrs. Astor on Fifth Avenue but not so appropriate for Mom and a two-year-old in Hope. However, they were accepted in the spirit in which they were given and I still have them. When my girls were little, they loved playing with their "Foxy-Loxies," which are yellowed and tattered now but still give me a warm feeling when I brush their tails across my chin.

Jimmy also brought a gift for Dad: a gorgeous gold nugget watch fob and chain. He had hidden it away in an old sock and then forgotten where he'd put it. When he came across it months later, he was afraid he'd lose it again, and since he didn't have any relatives to leave it to, he gave it to Dad. After Dad passed away, Mom and I had it made into a necklace, which we shared.

The Hope bachelors were good to us kids. There were so few of us that we were a precious commodity and were treated as such. Women and children were rare in that time and place. That made me feel special, and it was the beginning of my lifelong affection for, and appreciation of, the male animal. I'm glad "women's liberation" has other meanings, for I thoroughly enjoy men and have never felt a need or desire to be liberated from them.

Those old sourdoughs went out of their way to be patient and kind with us. I remember several dolls (including one with genuine beaver-pelt hair) that arrived at Christmas, and handmade toys as well, not to mention their tall tales of adventure that made our eyes pop.

After Willy left us, his tiny cabin was empty for only a short time. One day a man named Oscar showed up and moved in. Oscar was a nice old Scandinavian guy in his 70s, plump and pink-cheeked. In his younger days he had been a fisherman, trawling the fertile waters off Alaska. Now he received a small pension, and he cooked and puttered around for himself.

There were frequent potlucks in those days in the Hope Social Hall, a venerable building erected at the turn of the twentieth century and still in use in the twenty-first. These affairs were held at the slightest excuse and were usually followed by a dance. The old log walls of the hall fairly vibrated as sourdoughs, miners, trappers, and their women stomped and twirled to the tunes played by Bob Davis and Bob DeFrance on guitars, and Lewis Shell and Dennie McCart on violins. There were other amateur musicians from time to time, and whatever they lacked in talent they made up for in enthusiasm. Their audiences thought they were great.

Lewis Shell was a particular favorite of mine when I was a toddler. He was, I think, in his late teens, part Alaska Native. Whenever he took a break from the violin, he'd relax on one of the wooden benches lining the walls of the hall. As soon as he sat down, I'd sashay on over and plunk down beside him as close as I could snuggle. Embarrassed, he'd slide farther down the bench, and I'd scoot right after him. Finally he'd run out of bench and have to either return to the fiddle or we'd repeat the procedure on another bench. Shy Lewis!

A potluck marked Thanksgiving of the Black Winter of, I believe, 1941. A Black Winter is a winter without snow—a rarity in Alaska, but it does happen. It's thought to be a bad omen. The following summer is doomed to have more mosquitoes and no-see-ums, and other catastrophes are sure to accompany the ominous weather.

By that Thanksgiving there had been no snow, but winter was young. (It was not, technically, even winter yet.) Everyone gathered at the Hall for the potluck except Oscar, who wasn't feeling well and stayed home in Willy's little cabin. After dinner, Mom made up a plate of goodies and took it to him, but he didn't answer her knock. When she went into the cabin, she found him dead in his bunk. I think it was that same winter that Elmer Carson, the former Hope postmaster, died. I don't remember him in person but sure recognize him in photos. As I said, he had no legs. He scooted around on a little wagon and kept a short stool handy, onto which he hopped to sort mail and conduct business. The summer before he died, a bunch of us went up into the mountains to pick berries and get ice from a glacier to make ice cream for the Fourth of July town picnic. I have a photo of us with old Mr. Carson on that outing. He's sitting propped up on a blanket. At his funeral I was afraid to look at him in his homemade, half-sized coffin, as in my father's arms I passed by with the others to pay my last respects.

It might have been that winter that Pap Clark passed away, too. Pap's real first name was Hubbard; he was Emma's father-in-law, Carl and Earl Clark's father. The Clark family had come to Hope from Texas in 1913 and as noted were related somehow to the Mathisons. The matriarch of the family, called Granny by everyone in town, was a substantial woman with erect carriage, white hair, a twinkle in her eye and a wad of tobacco in her cheek. She had the Texan's talent for tall tales and liked to tell about the 1916 earthquake that hit Alaska like a bomb. The Clarks had an old truck parked on the hill in front of their house, and as the earth began to buck and heave, according to Granny, the truck rolled first up the hill, then back down, and finally came to rest at the top of the hill again. I remember that old truck. It had wheels with wooden spokes and a wooden steering wheel with a round button in the middle that gave a goose honk when pounded on. In my childhood, I doubt that the old wreck ever moved or even could move. We kids loved to play on and in it.

A few years after I was born, a missionary couple from Seward began coming to Hope every other week to hold services at Granny's house. They didn't have many takers: Emma, Granny, and my folks and I were just about it. Reverend Dean was a mighty preacher, and we sang hymns a cappella at the top of our lungs. I liked going to "church," but what I remember most is playing with Granny's little farm animal set, and the smell of Granny's house: homemade applesauce, decades of moosemeat roasts, dust, and tobacco juice in the spitcans.

I'd usually fall asleep and ride home on Dad's shoulder, safe in the knowledge that Jesus loved me and so did my parents. It seems as if I've always been a Christian. I asked the Lord to forgive my sins when I was a very small child, and I've loved Him and tried to follow His teachings all my life. I don't always succeed, but I try.

Actually, I was baptized three times. The first time (Methodist) was shortly after my birth. The second time was as a teenager, when our non-denominational missionary decided all Christian souls should make a reaffirmation of their faith (this accomplished in a very cold, slimy lake about 14 miles from Kenai). And the third time was after I was married, living in South Carolina and attending a Baptist church. Naturally, they insisted I be submerged yet another time.

Hope became part of the war effort when some Army people arrived from Seward and issued rifles and gas masks to everyone in the village. The Japanese had landed on Adak and Attu islands in the Aleutian chain, and some Hopeites claimed that light from their fires could be seen reflected off low-hanging clouds at night. It was feared that Hope would be in their path as they made their way to Anchorage, Alaska's largest city. A couple of spies had been caught in Seward, broadcasting reports to the Japanese over short-wave radios, and everybody who had any sense was getting fearful. Many Alaska families were being evacuated Outside for the duration. ("Outside" is an Alaskan term for the "Lower 48" states.) But in Hope we just sat tight.

Fortunately for me, I didn't have any sense. But I *was* afraid—of the ugly gas mask that hung over my crib. My very first memory is of that khaki-colored monstrosity with the buggy eyes and elephant's-trunk hose peering down at me as I lay trembling beneath the covers.

Annette ("Granny") Clark

Joyce Rheingans on a ride with Kent King

Picnic day: Elmer Carson, far left; back row, Flora McCart, baby Carla Mae Clark, Arlene Rheingans, Emma Clark; front, Berdie Clark, Dennie McCart

One pitch-black night as the town nervously slept, a horrendous explosion rocked our little home. Immediately a roaring fire lit up the cabin, and flames danced toward the ceiling. Dad leapt from the bed and grabbed his rifle, while Mom made a dash for my little closet-room. Suddenly, amid the fire and smoke and yelling (for they were sure the Japanese had captured us), all became still. They looked sheepishly at each other, and then Dad returned his rifle to the rack and Mom tucked me in once more beneath the leering gas mask. There was no "Yellow Horde" (the wartime term). Only a sooty old potbellied stove that had overheated and blown its lid sky-high.

The invasion never did come, and life continued to move along at a snail's pace in Hope.

The Army Engineers came to town the summer that I was three. They were handsome, fun-loving young fellows, far from homes and families, and I became their mascot. They spoiled me shamelessly. One of them had a new camera, so they posed me in corny postures and I did my best to amuse them. Some of the pictures show me with a pipe clamped in my teeth, a la General MacArthur, and in others I'm riding shotgun in their jeep. In most of their pictures I'm looking pretty goofy, so I suppose I was hamming it up. You may be sure that my mother had spit-shined and curled me to the nines, however. Dad was a little jealous of the attention these fellows paid his family, and he refused to go to the hall dance when they were there.

I loved to perform, and Mom loved to teach me "pieces." These were nursery rhymes, poems, jokes, Bible verses—anything that could be recited to an audience of one or more. By the time I was four, I could recite 25 Bible verses and name all the books of the Bible in order. At three I sang "White Christmas" at the school Christmas program, solo and sans accompaniment. It wasn't that I was so talented. I just had a lot of nerve, and Mom had far too much time on her hands. And, since the Hopeites were starved for entertainment, any offering was received with wild enthusiasm.

Auntie Emma Clark had two little girls, one around four years older than I and the other just 10 months older—Berdie and Carla Mae respectively. Little Carla was sweet and soft and placid, while Berdie was her father's child, beautiful and dark and wild as a Gypsy. Uncle Carl would egg her on, and she would do the most outlandish things. Emma couldn't control her worth a fig. If Emma told Berdie not to do something, that's exactly what Berdie wanted to do—and did. If she told Berdie not to touch something, that's what Berdie made a grab for. The only way Emma could keep Berdie away from anything was to put a large, framed picture of Eleanor Roosevelt in front of it. For some reason, Berdie was scared to death of Mrs. Roosevelt.

Berdie often ambled across the road to our place to visit. Mom wondered why, whenever Berdie came to call, I, a normally content and happy baby, would howl like a coyote. Then one day Mom caught Berdie red-handed. Quick as a flash, Berdie gave me a wicked pinch, and quicker than a flash, Mom popped Berdie a slap in the chops. She said it's the only time she ever hit someone else's child; we both felt-she was justified.

Ol' Berdie just got braver and wilder. We met again nearly 50 years after our last childhood encounter, and she had miraculously become a lovely, serene woman. But in her childhood, she was a holy terror. I can see her, for example, on the narrow log and plank bridge that crossed Resurrection Creek at Hope, near our cabin. Just wide enough for one small car, it had no sides or railings, just a 6-inch by 6-inch plank on either side. I had been warned often not to go near the creek, or the bridge, without permission, and when allowed to cross the bridge, only to walk directly down dead center.

The Clarks had built a large log cabin on "the hill"—the base of the mountain across the creek. Berdie would come tearing down the hill on her bike, hit the approach to the bridge, aim as close to the edge as possible and rip across while the creek below roared out to Turnagain Arm. Even the boys were in fear and trembling of Ol' Berdie. It's amazing how 50 years can change a person.

In the winter, Dad worked with Roy Mitchell for the Bureau of Public Roads, keeping the road between Hope and Moose Pass clear, but he also ran a few traplines to make some extra money. He'd "pick the traps" on the weekends, and bring home his catch: lynx, coyotes, rabbits, and my favorites, the snowy white ermine (weasels with their winter coats on). The animals were frozen stiff, in lifelike poses, and I became quite attached to them. Dad made the mistake of letting me play with a deceased weasel, solid as a Popsicle, and I wouldn't give it back. I carried it around until it thawed and got quite ripe, but by then Dad had caught a freshly frozen one, and I was willing to trade.

Erv and Arlene Rheingans—two winters, two lynx, two weasels

Winter, Hope, Alaska   1943 - '44
High Tide:- Turnagain Arm of Cook Inlet
    Our land flooded

Joyce + Erma Ann

Irv & Arlene
Reingans

Lewie & Ross
Miller

And so we bartered throughout the winter.

Almost as soon as I could walk, I got my first pair of ice skates. I presume they came from Sears or Wards, like most everything else we owned. They weren't shoe-skates, just a metal frame with straps you buckled around your boots or shoepacs. Because I was a wobbly beginner, mine had double blades the first few years, till I graduated to singles. As soon as the mudflats north of Hope flooded from a high tide and froze over, the whole town strapped on their skates and declared a holiday. Since it was winter and there wasn't much else to do in an Alaska mining town, we spent many happy hours on the ice.

Entire families, oldtimers, bachelor miners, all skated during the dim, dark days of winter. Babies were brought along, wrapped to their eyeballs in blankets and stuffed into wooden Blazo boxes nailed to sleds. Bearded men in woolen jackets and stocking caps pushed dog sleds (without the dogs) filled with laughing women and kids.

Sledding was another favorite winter sport. This involved a hike to the top of a long hill about a mile out of town. Given a little run and a push off, one could sled all the way into town. I remember doing this, again as a community activity, on moonlit winter nights. With the northern lights flashing and trees creaking and popping from the cold, we huffed and puffed our way up the hill and then came squealing down. The air was so cold it would frost the hairs in your nose and freeze your lungs if you breathed through your mouth. So you covered your entire face except for your eyes with a woolen scarf, put on several pairs of mittens (mine were Mom-knitted and joined by a long, braided yarn rope that ran from one mitten up through the sleeve of my coat to the other sleeve and mitten, the hope being to render them immune to loss), donned a pair of long johns, two sweaters, thick snowpants, two or three pairs of wool socks, shoepacs, and finally a heavy coat and a stocking cap with a fuzzy yarn pom-pon on top. God help you if you had to take a wee-wee during the next four or five hours. It simply wasn't done, or it wasn't done simply. This no doubt contributed to my remarkable bladder control in later years.

Sometimes old Mr. Buzard would give us kids a ride on his dog sled. Hitched to his team of huskies, we'd mush up and down the main street of Hope, having the time of our lives. Some sled dogs were quite tame, but many were vicious. If not fed enough, they have been known to kill and eat small animals that wander too near their staked territory; and in at least two cases I know of, small children were killed by sled dogs. We kids gave them the proper respect, and they gave us some thrilling rides.

Directly across from our cabin stood Doc (Iver) Nearhouse's store. It had formerly belonged to George Roll, but Doc took it over about the time I was born. Doc was a Santa Claus lookalike, without the beard. Rotund and merry, he lived above the store and presided over a vast array of "stuff." Canned food was stacked precariously on tottering shelves, huge slabs of mold-covered bacon hung from the rafters, cans of Blazo kerosene stood beside stacked boxes of shoepacs, which nestled against pairs of snowshoes. Snoose, cigarettes and other tobacco products were handy right behind the counter, while bins of flour, sugar and other staples required a cautious delving deep into the bowels of the store. Hairpins, soap products, face powder and Band-aids could eventually be found if you looked hard enough. I don't remember any perishables. There was no electricity in town, and certainly no refrigeration. The store produced a pungent, unforgettable aroma: part food-smell, part petroleum product, part animal, and over all a musty, dusty, "old" smell. It was a perfumed Aladdin's cave of goodies where Doc reigned supreme, assisted only by his huge yellow dog.

Doc, another hardy Norwegian, was originally named Iver Nernus and had studied to be a pharmacist in Washington state before the Alaska gold bug bit him. He'd run a drug store in Anchorage for a while, and although I don't think he found any more gold than anybody else in the '30s around Hope, he did have enough money to purchase the store from Mr. Roll, including the stock, some of which had probably been there since the turn of the century.

With the store, Doc got Mr. Roll's garden and orchard. Mr. Roll had prepared and tended these latter-day Edens over the years with much TLC and a heavy application of horse droppings. Should a horse or cow or bull (and Hope had a few) meander down the street in front of the store, out would rush Mr. Roll to scoop the poop with his snow shovel. The results were magnificent. Mr. Roll, and eventually Doc, grew the most gigantic vegetables, flowers, fruits and berries imaginable. Of course the rich, black, virgin Alaskan soil and the 24-hour summer sunshine had a lot to do with it, but the prime ingredient was, no doubt, the do-do.

Doc Nearhouse and Rex, at Doc's store

Arlene as General Douglas MacArthur

Auntie Emma Clark's flower garden was a close second. She followed Mr. Roll's example, and fortunately for her, Uncle Carl always had a horse or two around the place. Her house plants were particularly lush, but her home sometimes smelled a bit like the barn. Emma mixed the horse droppings with water and kept the solution handy for a quick botanical feeding whenever a posy looked slightly undernourished.

Since the nearest "real" doctor was in Seward, our Doc Nearhouse was often called upon to treat injuries and illnesses. He claimed to have delivered a baby and done minor operations, but I couldn't vouch for that. I do know that he saved my life.

One day when I was around two years old, my nose started bleeding. I don't know whether I'd ever had a nosebleed before, but for many years afterward, I had frequent and ferocious nosebleeds. They continued until after I was an adult, when a Chicago doctor cauterized a "bleeder" in my nostril. This one I was told was a doozy. Mom tried everything she could think of to stem the flow, and Emma wasn't able to turn me off, either. After all else failed, and with a still-draining kid on their hands, one of them ran across the street for Doc. He hustled over, assessed the situation, swooped me up under his arm and ran out the back door. As he lumbered past our woodshed, he yanked the ax from the chopping block and then dashed down to the creek, Mom panting along in his wake.

At the creek, Doc chopped a hole in the ice and began scooping up freezing water and ice chips in his big paw and applying them to the back of my neck and my nose. In due time the hemorrhage stopped, and I was returned dripping wet, half frozen and pale as a winter weasel to my mother's arms.

We were able to control most subsequent nosebleeds, though I did have to go to the hospital emergency room several times for treatment and gauze packing after I moved to the States. Doc's treatment worked as well as any, until the cauterizing finally cured me once and for all. Forty-nine years after that incident, I stood at Doc's grave in a rugged cemetery near the top of our old sledding hill and silently thanked him.

The creek was a mixed blessing. It was swift and quite deep in those days, more of a river than a creek, and Mom was terrified I'd fall in. When I was old enough to play outside, she devised a method to prevent this from happening. She attached one end of a long piece of rope to a bent nail on the wall of the cabin, and tied the other end securely around my chubby middle. Then she went into the house, confident that she had the problem, and me, under control.

Her peace of mind lasted about as long as it took her to get back inside. At precisely the moment she closed the door, I discovered, to my humiliation, that I was tied like a dog to a tether, and I let out a howl that could be heard on the other side of town. Mom briefly entertained the idea that I'd soon resign myself to my fate and give up the protestations. She can be excused for her ignorance; she'd only known me a couple of years.

My bellows easily outlasted her patience, and when it seemed likely that irate neighbors would soon arrive to investigate, she admitted defeat and unbound me. But she then proceeded to scare the very liver out of me regarding what would happen if I even considered venturing near the creek. She made a believer out of me—I developed an enormous respect for the creek. Parenthetically, my mom never learned to swim, and neither did I.

What Hope may have lacked in sophistication, it made up for in characters, both human and animal. We had many interesting neighbors. One was Peggy Nutter, who arrived with her husband and several children, including a set of twins, and pretty much bowled everybody over with her background, education and energy. She was a large woman, in every sense of the word. She had been involved in journalism in the States and was considered to be well-educated and erudite. But she didn't know beans about roughing it on the Last Frontier. She tried hard, though, and that first summer she put in a huge garden, which she tended faithfully.

Peggy also had a cow. She was determined that her children should have fresh milk, not the canned variety the rest of us choked down. (I learned to drink coffee before I started first grade, but it was laced with lots of Pet milk and sugar. It was the only way Mom could get that milk down me.) One lovely summer day, while Peggy was bending over pulling weeds in her garden, the cow became amorous, if a bit gender-confused. She took a look at Peggy's broad beam, snuck up on her and mounted her from the rear.

This experience was bad enough for Peggy on its own, goodness knows, but a couple of the miners were walking past and caught the whole act. In no time, word spread around town, and while the women giggled modestly, the men laughed and joked about it for months.

Long before white men came to wrest gold from the creeks and mountains, a small group of Athabaskan Indians, the Kniks, lived in the area around Hope. History tells us they often fought with the Tyoneks from across Cook Inlet; in any case, there was nothing left of their settlement by the 1930s except a couple of decaying shacks and a little burial ground on a point of land about a mile east of Hope.

We kids heard stories of how the Indians had "buried" their dead in wooden boxes in the branches of cottonwood trees, along with certain weapons, jewelry and other treasures. Several times we hiked over to Indian Point and snooped around hopefully, but we found only a few wooden planks up in the trees. I've read since that the actual graves were in the ground and that early white men had raided them long before our time, thus preventing us from becoming bona fide grave robbers.

The only Native or part-Native families in Hope that I remember were the Hatches, the Shells, and the Richards. One autumn morning as the days were growing shorter and colder, Dad was invited to go duck hunting with some of the Hatch men. Ducks and geese congregated by the thousands on the rich feeding grounds of Chickaloon flats, on their journey south for the winter. Dad and the Hatches shot a few more than they needed to take home and decided to make duck stew with the extras.

When the stew was ready, the men all squatted around the pot and simply reached in with their hands, grabbed whatever floated by and put it in their mouths. So many unwashed hands dunking into the pot put a crimp in Dad's appetite. Besides which, he was fastidious about his own hands. It always amazed and amused me that he could kill and dress a moose, plant a garden or overhaul an engine, but never get his hands dirty, or so it seemed. He always kept a rag handy on which to wipe them, and his fingernails and hands were always clean and white.

When young Uncle Willy was still with us, he had a go at hunting, too. He spotted what he believed to be the biggest goose he'd ever seen, took careful aim, and blew it into the hereafter. He proudly lugged this enormous bird back to town, only to be met with much scornful teasing. He had killed a swan by mistake. He felt so bad about it that he asked Mom to cook it so they could eat it and its death wouldn't have been in vain. Mom stuffed and roasted it, but it was too tough for human consumption; they had to give it to the dogs.

We depended on wild fowl and game for our food. It's a good thing that the men had lots of spare time in the winter and that most of them were good shots. I'm certain my dad was one of the best hunters in Alaska. He'd done his share of hunting in the north woods of Minnesota as a youth, and he could pick the eye out of a moose at a distance where many people couldn't even see the moose. He never earned much money, but he kept us well supplied with meat.

At that time most of the moose was canned and put away for later use, but some fine steaks were consumed early on, and a lot of the meat was ground up for hamburger. The very best part was eaten as soon as Dad returned from a successful hunt. He always brought the liver directly to Mom, so she could fry it up with lots of onions. It was still warm when it went into the frying pan, and when it was laid alongside a mound of mashed potatoes, well, you just don't eat any finer than that.

Somebody in Hope killed a bear one year and the meat wasn't bad, although bear can sometimes be too gamy to eat. No doubt it depends on what the bear has been eating: early spring berries or late fall salmon. I grew up thinking that bear is not your best meat for eating, unless you're very, very hungry and your chances of killing something better are very, very slim.

There were a lot of bears around Hope, though. The entire Kenai Peninsula abounds in both black and Kodiak brown bears, and many record-sized trophies have been taken there. Sometimes in the summer when we'd go up Palmer Creek to pick berries, we'd see black bears on the slopes of the mountains, rolling and tumbling and sliding down a grassy hill on their bottoms. Cubs are cute as can be, but they travel with overprotective, bad-tempered mamas.

One afternoon, the Boe kids and Leslie Brattain and I were invited to have a sleepover in the Clarks' barn with Berdie and Carla Mae. As I've mentioned, the Clarks had built on a hill across the creek, where besides their log home they had some outbuildings and a barn in which Uncle Carl kept a horse or two to haul logs, plow the garden, and provide the not-so-secret ingredient for Auntie Emma's premium flower fertilizer.

John Grueninger and Erv Rheingans with ducks and coyote

Arlene and Pepsi the cat

That evening we climbed into the hayloft, snuggled into our sleeping bags, and proceeded to sleep the sleep of the innocent. All night the horses were noisy and restless, but Uncle Carl assumed it was because we were making them nervous. We kids heard nothing. In the morning, when he came to wake us, Carl found fresh bear tracks all around the barn, even on an old car that was parked beside it.

Everybody in town had outdoor toilets. Some were fancier than others. Ours, you will recall, had a fur-lined seat. Every decade or so, the pit would fill up and the man of the house would have to dig a new hole and cover the old mess over with the dirt. Uncle Carl had done his share of toilet-hole digging, so when they moved up on the hill, he decided to build his privy on stilts, sort of hanging over the side of the hill, thus eliminating the need for a pit. He later said the arrangement worked just fine until Doc started stocking toilet tissue in the store and Emma had to have some. One day the wind blew up from below, and when Carl threw the used toilet paper down the hole, it blew back up and wrapped around his neck. He said he preferred the old catalogues anyway.

Besides Uncle Carl's horses, he kept a bunch of sled dogs, and usually a lynx or two in a pen. Most families had sled dogs. Peggy Nutter had her amorous cow, of course, and Kent King kept an enormous red bull out on his homestead a mile or two from town. On occasion, Kent would hitch this bull to a wagon and drive into town, and sometimes he gave the locals free rides.

One day a small airplane landed on the mudflats north of Hope. The pilot tied it down and hied over to the store to conduct a little business. Unfortunately, that's the day the red bull got loose. He meandered over to the flats and—possibly mistaking the plane for a Japanese fighter—attacked it. The bull darn near demolished the thing before he could be subdued.

When I was a few years old, I was given a kitten which we named Pepsi-Cola, or just plain Pepsi for short. As cats go, this one was extremely bright—and cooperative and chummy, a rarity in ordinarily standoffish felines. Pepsi and I played hide and seek. I'd go hide and she'd come find me, and sometimes we would reverse the process. Whichever, as soon as we'd spy each other, Pepsi would make a flying leap and land, clinging to my chest. Remarkably, she never scratched me but knew exactly how far to sink her claws into my shirt or sweater. I had a homemade wooden jeep that I pulled around on a string, and when Pepsi was small, she loved to sit on the jeep and ride. Before long, though, she grew too big to sit on the jeep, so she'd just put her front paws on it and hop along behind as I toddled around the cabin.

You can't exactly classify them as animals, but the infamous, voracious, ferocious Alaskan mosquitoes were, without fear of contradiction, the most prevalent critters around. I don't know how we survived them. It's a good thing they attack only in the summertime, or I doubt Alaska would ever have become settled. On many occasions I was so covered with mosquito bites that my eyes were swollen almost shut. Even now, I'm a lobster dinner to a mosquito. I've been with groups when nobody else got a nibble, while I've been practically gnawed to the bone. And I don't want to hear anything about "stinging," either. I know a bite when I get one. For most of my childhood, I was slightly lumpy all summer long, decorated with crusty white blobs of dried baking soda.

*Joyce, Arlene and Erv Rheingans on a fishing trip up Resurrection Creek
(Ed Rust is standing in the background)*

6

WHEN I WAS THREE AND A HALF OR SO, my pal Shirley Boe's father, Homer, moved his family to Seward so he could work on the docks, longshoring. My folks perceived this as a way for us to make some money, too, so we followed the Boes to Seward.

We didn't live there very long, but Mom remembered Seward as a wild and woolly little seaport, full of miners, trappers, Natives, GIs and construction workers besides the founding families that had been there for several decades. Businessman John Paulsteiner wrote a book titled *Seward, Alaska, the Sinful Town on Resurrection Bay,* which she thought pretty much said it all.

Mom was hired to manage a rooming house on Fifth Avenue called the Portland Arms, and we moved into one of the apartments there. Again she really had her hands full, keeping 10 rooms, the lobby, and our apartment clean. That doesn't mean she let up on me, though. Pictures show me still curled and in fresh, pretty dresses and Mary Janes, and I continued to recite, sing and perform for anybody who would sit still for it, apparently earning a small reputation as the Portland Arms' own Shirley Temple in the process.

I was rewarded for my efforts with more candy and other treats than Mom thought were good for me. She solved the problem by surreptitiously pinning a neatly printed sign to the back of my dress:

DO NOT FEED OR GIVE ME CANDY.

I have a memento of our time in Seward. One day while playing by the train depot, I found along the track a beautiful teardrop-shaped piece of ivory. Mom had a gold nugget attached to the piece and had it made into a necklace for me.

We stayed in Seward for only about six months. Then work on the docks became scarce, and my folks had had just about all they could stomach of "the sinful town on Resurrection Bay." The weather was turning cold and the renters were firing up their room heaters to the red-hot stage. After several nearby buildings burnt to the ground, Mom and Dad decided we shouldn't press our luck. We returned to our little cabin in Hope, with a few dollars put aside.

Arlene in the park near the Seward railroad depot, with a bunny on the loose

Erv Rheingans at the Bureau of Public Roads shop at Moose Pass

The Mitchell family: Roy, Alice with Martha, Betty, Harvey

Dad resumed working for the Bureau of Public Roads, with Roy Mitchell. Roy's wife, Alice, was our postmaster after Mr. Carson passed away. I played with their little girl, Martha Ann, but my best bud was Shirley Boe, and not just because of her handsome older brother, Gene, whom I secretly adored. The Boes had abandoned Seward for the time being also.

Martha Ann was quite a visitor. She'd just appear in your house, unannounced and without so much as a rap at the door. Mom always made her go back out, knock, and wait for a cheerful "Come in," but the next time there she was again, like a little apparition. Alice finally had to pin a note on her clothes, too: SEND ME HOME AT 4 P.M., else Martha Ann would have visited all night.

One day Shirley, Martha Ann and I went to visit Dennie McCart's pretty young wife, the former Flora Shell. Flora, like so many Alaska Natives, had contracted tuberculosis, and she was dying. Dennie writes about our visit in *The Hope Truckline*.

> These three little girls, Martha, Shirley and Arlene, got a
> big kick out of climbing over the stile at the fence
> between Mitchells' and my place, and this day they
> stopped in to visit Flora. Arlene was looking all around
> the room, scared, so Flora asked her what was wrong.
> Arlene said, "I am not supposed to be in your house. You
> have germs, but I don't see any." Bless her little heart. It
> did strike Flora kind of funny, and she got a big laugh
> out of it. When I got home that night she had to tell me
> about the visit.

I'm sure not proud of that little story, but it shows how hard my mother tried to keep me from harm's way. It didn't always work, though, and I have healed scars on one lung from a mild case of TB that we weren't even aware I had at the time.

Mom always was a fussbudget, and she did enjoy fussing with me. I can understand it now: her lack of companionship, the boredom, the loneliness and isolation. But in those days I wasn't always the cooperative little dolly. A couple of times the schoolteacher brought her little boy over to play. We were about three or four years old, and those silly mothers made us dress up in each other's clothes. To me this little boy was suspect anyway, as he had long, white-blond curls, longer and curlier than mine, ditto his eyelashes. I didn't like him one bit, and I didn't like wearing his little soldier suit, either. In the pictures we have, I'm scowling like a prune, and he's looking pleased as punch in my favorite pink dress.

Dad was transferred to the Bureau of Public Roads shop in Moose Pass, so we left Hope for a while when I was four-going-on-five. We rented a house in Moose Pass from Lyle and Louise Saxton, and I got acquainted with a whole new batch of friends.

On my fifth birthday, Mom threw a party for me and invited all the kids in town, probably about 15 in all. I don't like parties now, and I didn't like parties then. As I recall, everyone had a wonderful time, with the possible exception of my mother and me: I hid under her bed and wouldn't come out until it was time for presents and cake.

It was in Moose Pass that I learned about the birds and the bees. I asked, and Mom told! I thought it was just about the grossest thing I'd ever heard, and I ran away from home until hunger overcame my disgust and I showed up for dinner, willing to forgive my parents for their revolting behavior.

You may wonder why Mom told such a young child the unvarnished truth. Well, when she was a girl, nobody told her anything about s e x, but they did tell her about Santa Claus and the Easter Bunny. She felt so stupid when she finally learned the truth—nearly in her teens—that she swore she would never lie to *her* children. Except for my initial trauma, I've always appreciated her frankness and admired her attitude regarding honesty.

When school started that fall, I'd just turned five. The teacher, a "maiden lady" named Miss Clark (no relation to the Hope Clarks), invited me to come to school with the rest of the kids, and I was thrilled. On the first day of school, though, I couldn't open the front door and had to trudge back home to get my mom. I loved going to school, but somebody ratted on me to the Board of Education in Juneau, and presently Miss Clark received a letter informing her that the legal age for school was six. I was banished in tears. The week before my woeful dismissal, we heard on the teacher's radio that President Franklin Roosevelt had died at the southern White House in Georgia. We were immediately released from school, and I can

Fifth birthday party in Moose Pass, June 1944

Arlene, left, and visitor in swapped clothes

recall how important I felt arriving home as the bearer of such momentous tidings.

One of my best friends in Moose Pass was a boy named Bobby who lived a couple blocks from us, on the outskirts of town. One day as I was waiting across the road from his house for him to come out and play, I walked over to the edge of the road, a high, but gradual, weedy slope down to a rocky beach and the lake. There I had the surprise of my young life. Running along the beach was a young woman with extremely long, brilliantly auburn hair flowing out behind her as she ran. She was dressed so strangely: purple and pink gossamer garments billowed behind her, and oddest of all, a turban was wound about her head. I was flabbergasted. Since I knew everybody in town, I couldn't imagine who it might be, and I'd never before (nor since) seen such clothing. I've often wondered who or what I saw that day. Maybe it was one of those supernatural experiences . . . a ghost, or an angel, or an extra-terrestrial. If so, I sure wish she'd show herself again, because I've got lots of questions for her.

While we were in Moose Pass, Dad started feeling poorly. He went to the doctor in Seward and was told that he should get Outside to the best hospital he could find. To Dad's way of thinking, that would be the Mayo Clinic in Rochester, Minnesota.

Off we went. When I asked in later years how my folks afforded that trip, I was told they were able to save money from Dad's Bureau of Public Roads job. Mom says there wasn't anything to spend the money on except a minimal rent, and a few staples. At any rate, we caught the first available Alaska Steamship out of Seward.

The war was still on, so these ships were also used as troop carriers. What a marvelous trip I had. The soldiers were excited and happy to be finished with duty in remote Alaska, and as I was the only child aboard they spoiled me terribly. But I became such a pest, interrupting their poker games and begging for stories and songs, that they eventually lost patience and decided to get rid of me for a while.

"How would you like to go snipe hunting?" one of the boys asked. Hunting! Oh boyoboyoboy! My dad was a great hunter, and now somebody was suggesting that I go hunting, too. I could hardly believe my ears, and it was hard to wait until after dinner, which, coincidentally, was when most of the card games got down to serious business.

At last it was time for me to take my position. The guys provided me with a brown paper bag and got me situated below deck, squatting at ready behind a dark metal staircase. They admonished me to be very, very quiet while I held the bag open between my feet and waited for them to scout out the snipes and drive them in my direction.

I held my breath and tried to quiet my pounding heart as I squatted, then knelt, and finally sat on my fanny and waited for the herds of snipe to come stampeding toward me. Actually, I was a little scared, as I had neglected to ask just what exactly snipe were, and had no idea if they were fish, fowl or four-legged furries. And I wasn't sure what to do with them once I'd bagged my limit.

The GIs had told me that it might take a while to round up the snipes, so I waited as patiently as I could for as long as I could. Finally, very disappointed, cramped and quite a bit frustrated, I left my cubbyhole and marched up to the lounge area, crumpled paper bag in hand.

As I approached the open door to the lounge, laughter and bits of conversation came to my ears. I soon realized that I'd been had. Angry and embarrassed? You bet. I think at that moment a chunk of innocence fled my soul, and I was never again *quite* as gullible. It was a good joke, but I took it seriously. It was some time before the fellows could make amends, but I soon forgave them and resumed my pampered existence, sadder but wiser.

Because we were at war and Japanese submarines were believed to be a constant threat, our ship's portholes were covered over with blackout paint. No lights were to show at night—not even a cigarette lit on deck. We took part in frequent surprise lifeboat drills. I'd drop whatever I was doing and rush to my station, where somebody would enfold me in a bright orange Mae West jacket and we'd stand awaiting the "all clear." I don't remember being the least bit frightened. I knew my heroes would rescue me if my parents couldn't.

The crossing to Seattle took five days, and then we had to make our way by train to Minnesota. This was especially hard on Mom. I usually got a seat because I was a little kid, and Mom insisted Dad take any other available seat because he was so ill. There were very few civilian spaces available, and all trains were crowded with boys in uniform. Mom sat on a suitcase or stood in the aisle. The GIs were a

Wartime portrait—Joyce, Arlene and Erv Rheingans

keyed-up bunch, noisy, singing, playing cards and guitars, perhaps acting tough to cover up their apprehension. Able-bodied civilians were expected to defer to them. Occasionally one of the guys would get up to go to the bathroom or visit a buddy, and Mom would flop into his vacant seat for a few minutes' rest. The trains were hot and filthy, with scratchy, velvet-like seats that attracted soot from the windows opened for ventilation. It was a miserable four days to Minneapolis.

The folks farmed me out with relatives in and around Appleton, while they tried to get into the Mayo Clinic in Rochester, about 190 miles away. The clinic was full and there was a waiting list, so eventually they went to the University Hospital in Minneapolis instead. There Dad had prostate surgery. He had complications with hemorrhaging and had to return to the hospital, but eventually he began feeling better.

This trip was short, only a couple of months, but it afforded me the opportunity to meet my only living grandparent, Grandma Doring, my mother's mother, and many relatives whom I recognized immediately from photos in our album at home. I was treated as something of a novelty by my farm cousins. They called me "the Eskimo," which I didn't like one bit, although at that time I'd never even seen an Eskimo. A few years later, when I became friends with an Eskimo family, I realized that my cousins had unwittingly paid me a compliment. Despite the teasing, I loved being around my relatives and thoroughly enjoyed farm life.

But soon Dad wanted to get back to Alaska. Mom hoped he'd give up on the idea and stay in Minnesota, but Dad was hooked on Alaska. He set his face, and consequently our faces, too, toward the midnight sun.

We sailed from Seattle on another steamship that doubled as a troop and munitions carrier. This one had carried both petroleum products and fish oil, and still smelled of both. Because of "enemy activity," we had to take the Outside Passage, which was experiencing severe storms and high seas. It was no pleasure cruise. Everyone on board, including the officers and stewards, was seasick for five days.

I shared a stateroom with a young schoolteacher, while my folks suffered across the hall. Occasionally, Mom would stumble over to my room, swab the vomit and crud off me and then reel back to her own bed. It really didn't matter that the cooks were sick, too, since nobody had an appetite. One of the young stewards took pity on me. He'd open the door and throw packages of saltine crackers and chocolate bars on my bed once or twice a day. Hunger finally drove me to nibble some of the candy, which only served to give my up-chuck a rich, brown, rancid flavor.

During this horrible trip I had a strange dream, in segments. In my misery, I fell asleep and dreamed I was ice skating along a long, narrow creek. On the shore ahead there was a house or cabin. Then I woke up and coated the sheets with chocolate sauce. I fell back to sleep, only to pick up the dream right where it had left off. The house was still ahead of me on the creek bank. I skated on and the house grew closer. Again I awoke, spewed chocolate and went back to sleep. Once again the dream continued, this time with the house directly opposite me. This continued three or four times, and made such an impression that I've never forgotten it.

We somehow survived the trip. But by the time our ship came into port at Seward, Dad was feeling terrible again, and not just from seasickness, either. Dr. Bannister gave him a series of penicillin shots that helped, and we made our way back to our cabin in Hope.

Whatever was wrong with Dad, it got worse. By spring he was in really bad shape. Dr. Bannister strongly recommended Mayo Clinic, and my folks felt they had no choice.

None of us wanted to get on a ship again, but there was no other way Outside. And so we repeated the whole saga. The crossing was calm, but Dad was very sick and weak, and Mom literally had both of us on her hands, as well as having to carry the luggage when we hustled from ship to train to train to train. It was a nightmare deja vu: soldier boys everywhere, and hot, crowded, dirty trains and stations. At one layover we slept in the station overnight, my folks each in an army wheelchair and I on a field gurney.

At last we arrived back in Minnesota. I stayed with relatives again, sometimes with Grandma Doring, while my folks spent several weeks at Mayo Clinic. Both of them underwent myriad tests, for by now Mom was having migraine headaches. It was decided that the headaches were an inherited condition; several of Mom's siblings, as well as her grandmother, suffered from them. She learned to live with

Grandma Mary Ruby Morris Doring

Aunt Ivy Morris, about 1911

them for many, many years, but thankfully, the migraines eventually lessened to ordinary headaches.

Dad had to have another operation, very similar to the one he had endured the year before. This time they found a diverticulum on his bladder that was so large, doctors thought at first he had two bladders. It was positioned in such a way that they couldn't remove it, but they drained and treated it with medication and released him. We often wondered if a kick he received from a horse when he was a teenager, or perhaps the infamous dragline incident, might have caused his problems.

No matter what anybody said, Dad was convinced he had inoperable cancer. I believe this conviction stayed with him the rest of his life. Although he lived another 27 years, he was positive that the grim reaper was just around the corner. It seemed as if the oomph went out of his life, and he became more and more introverted and less and less involved with life. We never knew if he really felt that bad all those years, or if he was just calmly sitting there waiting for the cancer to get him, but there were very few things that interested him after that. I was not one of them.

While the folks were spending those miserable weeks at Mayo, I was having a grand time on the farm with various relatives, including Grandma Doring. She was a wonderful old lady who looked exactly like a grandma should: short, chubby, apple-cheeked, pug-nosed, bespectacled and aproned. She didn't have many teeth, her voice was sort of crackly, and she loved to argue. Since she'd raised nine kids, there wasn't much I could do to shock or surprise her, though I certainly tried. She seemed to enjoy having a child around again, and her patience was quite remarkable.

One time though, I overdid it. She asked what I wanted for breakfast, and I said, "A raw egg." She sniffed, "Nobody eats raw eggs." "My mother never cooks eggs," I insisted. "We always eat 'em plain." After arguing about it long enough to see that neither of us was going to win that one, Grandma said, "OK, here's your plain egg," and she cracked an egg into a blue bowl and put it under my nose. I was horrified, but manfully tried to get the slimy thing down. That day I learned that raw eggs and soft-boiled eggs look exactly alike from the outside, but very different on the inside. I also learned not to push Grandma too far.

Sometimes I slept with her. She was so chubby, she'd sink down into the mattress and I'd roll over on top of her as she slept, soft as a marshmallow in her voluminous flannel nighty. She'd make funny noises with her mouth as she was falling asleep, and as her muscles relaxed, she'd jump and twitch in a fascinating fashion. I always tried to stay awake for this show but didn't often outlast her.

She told great stories, for she was part Irish, and I think they are the best storytellers. She had enough superstition and imagination to be interesting, but she also had a very realistic, no-nonsense side to her. Her best stories involved ghosts and banshees and mysterious bumps in the night, but somehow I had the feeling that she herself took them with a large grain of salt.

One of Grandma's younger sisters, Ivy, was a story all by herself. Pretty and smart, as a child she was spoiled by their parents to the extent that she always had the finest clothes, preferential treatment, and even her own little pony and cart in which to drive to school. She possessed a beautiful contralto singing voice, which, combined with her vivid imagination and love of storytelling, made her very popular with the other schoolchildren. I don't suppose the pony cart hurt any, either. Ivy had everything going for her when she graduated from high school and set off for Washington, D.C., to work "for the government."

Nobody ever learned quite what happened, but a few years after her arrival in the capital, she jumped out of a second-story window and broke her leg. Speculation had it that Ivy had experienced a broken heart along with the broken leg. At any rate, her papa had to go get her and bring her home. She was a changed person. She'd sit in a rocking chair and rock back and forth, giggling to herself, and as the years went by she grew quite insane and eventually had to be put into an asylum.

When I stayed with Grandma, Ivy was still living with another of their sisters, though Grandma had kept her for a long time. I saw her only once and don't remember the incident, but I'll always remember the stories Mom told me about the strange things Ivy did. As a young girl, Mom had to sleep with Ivy, and she remembered well her quirks.

Ivy often wandered away from home and once walked clear to Appleton, carrying a black box under her arm. She took the box to a local lawyer and told him it contained evidence of a murder. Now this guy must have been totally lacking an inquisitive gene, for he told Ivy to take her box and go home—and he didn't even look inside, to my everlasting frustration. Because Ivy was rather fixated on murders (could her Washington experience have included murder so dire?), nobody paid any attention to her when she hinted darkly about bodies being buried in the south field of her father's farm.

All during my school years, whenever I was required to compose a story for literature class, I would fall back on Aunt Ivy and the mysterious black box. It was an easy "A."

Grandma seemed to harbor some concern that I, at age five, might have inherited Ivy's proclivity for madness. I suppose my Shirley Temple imitations and my fondness for adult companionship seemed odd to her. She wasn't used to only children who had imaginary companions instead of brothers and sisters. She warned my mom, "You'd better watch her—she might turn out just like Ivy."

I was secretly a little pleased at the time to be in such interesting company, but for the rest of my life, there's always been a little niggling fear at the back of my mind that I might turn out "just like Ivy." It's strange that at a particularly troubled time in my life I should run to Washington, D.C., and there find my destiny.

A lovely porcelain German doll of Ivy's was given to my mom, who gave it to me, and it now sits in our guest room. I have an unexplainable protective attachment to that doll, but my children were always afraid of her.

During the weeks I spent on the farm, I learned about some new animals. At least they were new to me. I was accustomed to weasels and lynx and bear and moose but didn't know much about horses and cows and pigs. Uncle Carl's horses were kept in the pasture up on the mountain and rarely seen in Hope, and Peggy's randy cow hadn't lasted long. So farm animals were a fascination, and I had to learn the hard way at times.

Uncle John raised prize purebred Black Angus cattle which he showed at the county and state fairs. I attended one of those fantastic carnivals and was thrilled by the 4-H kids who paraded their beautiful animals in the center ring. How I envied them! When we got back to Uncle John's, I begged to be allowed to lead a frisky little bull calf around on a rope. Uncle John pointed out that this little fellow hadn't been trained to walk with a leash, but I was persistent. I could be pretty pesky when I made up my mind, and Uncle John, being a bachelor and not used to little girls in his barn, finally lost patience.

He tied a rope around the little bull's neck, wrapped the other end around my hand, and we began our promenade. At first the calf wouldn't move, so I pulled and tugged until he got the idea. Only he got the idea too well. He moved. Oh boy, did he ever move. With a flick of his tail and a kick of his heels, he took off—a small freight train, dragging me along like a caboose. Before long I fell, and from then on it's all a blur of sharp pointed hooves, mud, cow dung and burned palms.

On another occasion, I'd gone to visit Glen's family. Glen's dad was my dad's cousin, which made Glen my second cousin, I guess. He was a teenager, strong and tanned from working on the farm, and I thought he was wonderful. I tagged him around, getting in the way, asking goofy questions. In the barn he cornered a little field mouse, which I insisted would make an excellent pet. Glen picked the mouse up in his big, gloved hands and let me touch its soft gray fur. Maybe it reminded me of my dead weasel pets. Anyway, I pleaded to hold the little mouse. Glen demurred. I begged some more: please, please, oh please! And Glen handed me the mouse. A live mouse, unlike a dead weasel, can bite. And it did. Hard.

Another time I visited my Aunt Thelma's family on their farm near Hutchinson. Aunt Thelma, Mom's older sister, had six kids, all a good bit older than I, and all used to a rough-and-tumble, give-as-good-as-you-get sibling existence. This crew was a bit overwhelming, and to top it off, they called me the Little Eskimo. On their farm was a lake they used for fishing and swimming. They all could swim, but I'd never had an opportunity to learn and was afraid of the water. One hot, humid Minnesota day, after chores were done, we all went swimming. They dove right off the dock into the deep water, while I waded and splashed along the shore, ankle deep in muck and algae. Occasionally I'd brave a dunk down into the brown water up to my neck. When we all climbed back out, I was aghast to find my body covered with slimy, odious bloodsuckers. Slurping away at my hide like icky brown Hoovers, they writhed and wiggled as I danced and yowled. My cousins, of course, considered this great entertainment.

I don't think any of these relatives meant to be cruel. I imagine they thought I was a bit prissy, with my curls and ruffled pinafores,

Rheingans siblings in Appleton, Minn., mid-1940s: from left, standing, the author with father Erv Rheingans , Lillian Lindahl, Helen Rice, Alice (Leets) Randleman, Alvina Shipley; squatting: Erlean Ernst and Willard ("Uncle Willy") Rheingans. Missing from the photo are sister and brother Esther Sieber and Rudolph Rheingans, then living in Salinas, Calif.

Uncle Donovan Doring with Joyce and Arlene Rheingans, Fort Leonard Wood, Mo.

and no doubt thought I was spoiled. It's a foregone conclusion that "only children" are spoiled, isn't it? I think they did find me and my Alaskan background a novelty, and I like to think they were just trying to include me in their activities, and perhaps educate me in the process. I did learn that I do not enjoy handling mice, frisky young cattle or leeches, so to that extent they were successful. I never stayed mad at them because I was so thrilled to be like normal people and have relatives.

A word on behalf of "only children": I take vehement exception to the notion that they're all spoiled. In my case, it's true my mother lavished a great deal of love, time and attention on my small person. She wanted me to look and act nice, and to be intelligent and well-mannered. Nothing wrong with that—I felt the same way about my TWO children. And in order to accomplish this, she had to keep me in line. I got my share of spankings and "good talking-to's," as well as her undivided attention to my hair and clothes and the state of my toilette. I really tried to please her, both because I loved her so much and because even at a very early age, I felt a responsibility to do my best because I *was* an only child. I knew she meant well and had my best interests at heart. I wasn't allowed to talk loudly, butt into adult conversations or talk back. Not that I didn't try. I did try, but was faithfully and consistently corrected. If Mom didn't immediately correct me, Dad looked at me. That's it. He just looked at me. That was enough to snap me back into shape.

I was taught the Golden Rule and all ten of the commandments, and was expected to live accordingly. I knew that I was accountable for my actions not only to my parents but to God Himself, which probably kept me out of a lot of trouble later on in life.

I'll admit to being a wee bit precocious and enjoying having an audience, but I took to heart my dad's admonition, "Don't make a spectacle of yourself." I probably received more than my share of attention, but I didn't have a lot of material things. My parents encouraged reading, games and creative activities. As I got older, I was expected to pull my own weight in church, school and civic activities. I was expected to contribute to the world.

If this sounds like a spoiled only child, I plead guilty.

After Dad's operation at Mayo Clinic my folks decided to stay in Minnesota. I think they were concerned about returning to Alaska, so far from top-notch medical attention, when Dad was still feeling so poorly.

They bought a small house in Appleton, Mom went to work at the local J.C. Penney store, and it looked as if we were going to settle in for good. The war was drawing to a close, but Mom's younger brother, my Uncle Donnie, had been called back overseas as a lieutenant in the Army. He and his pretty wife, Valborg, were living at Ft. Leonard Wood, Missouri, and she was expecting their first child. It was decided that Mom should travel to Missouri and escort Val back home to Minnesota, as she was having a difficult pregnancy.

Mom thought it best that I come along, so we set off on one of those wretched, over-crowded troop trains again. Conditions and connections were horrible, made worse by the oppressive Midwestern heat and humidity.

In the Minneapolis train station, crowds of pushing, sweating people, mostly men, strained at the gates in order to rush onto the train and get a seat when departure time came. Finally, the huge metal gate was opened, the mob surged forward and we were swept toward the train. In the commotion, I was torn from Mom's grasp. She was pushed out onto the platform, while I was left inside the station. And the railway official slammed the gate closed again, effectively shutting off the avalanche of people hoping to board the train. I was lost in the crush.

Like stampeding buffalo, the herd carried Mom farther down the platform, but she was feisty. She turned and pushed right back, yelling at the top of her lungs and battling her way for all she was worth. When she finally reached the gates, she jumped up and down and screamed until she caught the eye of the official, who wasn't about to open those gates again for anyone. The crowd inside the station was in near panic to get aboard the train, which was already full to capacity. With both Mom and me bawling and leaping about frantically, the poor man finally had an inspiration. He swept me up and literally threw me over the high gates into Mom's arms, and we fought our way onto the crowded train.

I don't remember anything else about the trip, except that unbelievable Missouri heat. At my uncle's quarters, I'd wash my dolly's clothes, run around the block just once, waving them like a fan, and they'd be completely dry. The trip back to Minnesota a few days later was even worse, as Val had awful morning sickness all the way and was so unhappy to be separated again from Donnie. We finally made it home safely, and so, thank the Lord, did Uncle Donnie and my other uncles who served in World War II.

I started first grade in Appleton, in the same school my mom and many other relatives had attended. Compared to the little one-room school in Hope, the Appleton school was huge, with several hundred pupils to the dozen or so in Hope.

Appleton, a small farming community with only one block of downtown stores, served the farm families in the southwestern corner of Swift County, Minnesota. It's the closest town to the farms of my parents' families, and it was on Appleton's little main street that Mom and Dad met in 1927, when she was a sophomore in high school and he had just returned from an exciting sojourn in California. In the Appleton cemetery rest four or five generations of my family, both Dorings and Rheingans, amid tombstones reflecting a strong German and Norwegian population.

Most people who lived in Appleton when we moved there had been there all their lives, and most of them apparently didn't have the slightest desire to live anywhere else. It was a nice, quiet, WASP-ish sort of town where everyone knew everyone else, and a good many of them were related, one way or the other. One of my mother's cousins was the mayor, my Uncle Willy would soon become the town policeman, and Uncle Donnie was eventually part owner of the local Chevrolet agency.

Venerable elm trees lined the residential streets, and at one end of town stood a tall metal flour mill alongside a nifty little pond and spillway. I was delighted to be living in Appleton, and Mom was, too.

Among my new friends was a little girl named Ruthie and a chubby little boy named Michael, who asked me to marry him as we returned home from school one day. I don't remember my answer, but it was probably a delighted "Yes!"

During first grade I took piano lessons from the wife of a prominent citizen. A cultured, buxom lady, Mrs. M. always bid me a fond "Toodle-ooo" as she waved good-bye from her doorway. I thought she was the height of elegance, and practiced trilling "Toodle-oooooo" in my own most refined tones.

First grade came easily for me, since I already knew my alphabet and numbers and could read fairly well. I received a little pin for good penmanship, and was inordinately proud of it. Unfortunately, my penmanship never seemed to improve after the first grade. My lame excuse is that for several years I attended school in a building in Alaska that was so blamed cold, I kept my mittens on most of the time.

It's surprising to me now that even my first-grade penmanship was considered good, because I was ambidextrous, using both hands equally. I was perfectly happy with the arrangement, but my teacher suggested that I select one hand and stick with it. I don't recall any pressure to choose the right hand over the left, but before long, the right became dominant and any plans to become a southpaw were scrapped.

At any rate, it's a good thing school was so easy, because I was absent quite a bit with a sore throat and earaches. Earlier, while still at Grandma's, I had had a miserable spell of illness and was so weak and tired for several weeks that I could barely get off the couch. There were frightful epidemics of polio, then usually called infantile paralysis, during those years, and my family worried that I might be coming down with that dread disease. Later it was thought it might have been a touch of rheumatic fever, for I was diagnosed as having a hole in my heart, or this may have been when I had the mild case of TB that showed up later as scars on my lung. Whatever it was, I recovered nicely but then began suffering from tonsillitis. Thus the sore throat and earaches. It wasn't my year.

I'd come dragging home from school so miserable I thought I'd die along the way. Mom or Dad would warm some mineral oil in a spoon, drop it from an eyedropper into my aching ears, and then plug them with wads of cotton. This did very little good, and eventually the doctor decreed that the tonsils had to come out. He wouldn't do it in the summertime, as that's when the polio bug was more likely to attack, so I had to suffer through several months more until the weather cooled.

Mom knew I wasn't going to let somebody cut my throat if I had any say in the matter. She dreaded taking me to the hospital on the date set for my surgery. Debating how she should handle the situation, and me, she finally hit upon a plan. Subterfuge. Pure and simple.

As luck would have it, an uncle was in the hospital at the time, so Mom told me we were going to visit him. Not *exactly* a lie. She and Dad dragged their heels as I skipped, carefree and ignorant, up the sidewalk to the Appleton Hospital. While Dad and I visited Uncle John in his room, Mom slipped out to tell the doctor I was there for my tonsillectomy. Unknown to her, I followed along and hid behind some large potted plants as she talked with the surgeon.

Apparently there wasn't any cotton in my ears that day, because I heard their foul plot, and they heard my reaction. She knew her little girl: I wasn't happy. But after a lot of blubbering, some calm reasoning, and yes, a bit of bribery, I accepted my fate. I stripped, donned a miniature hospital gown, and reluctantly conceded. The doctor carried me into the operating room, and I remember fretting that my bare bottom might show through the vent in the back of the gown. For a moment, that thought took precedence over the idea of having my throat cut.

Mom had promised that if I was a good girl and breathed very deeply into the ether cone, I would go to sleep and not feel a thing. To cinch the deal, I would awaken to find a new baby doll in bed with me (the implications of which are rather boggling), and would, in addition, have all the ice cream I could eat, that time-honored carrot at the end of the surgical stick. I wisely decided that since I was going to lose the battle, I might as well do it with some class and receive a nice reward in the bargain. As soon as they strapped me onto the operating table and clamped the cone on my face, I sucked in that ether in great, snorting gulps. Dad later said he could hear my gasps in a room two doors away.

I can't tell you anything about the surgery, except that I had a rather intriguing dream. I saw myself standing in a large, empty area. Coming toward me was a train-like vehicle, consisting of bright one-dimensional triangles, lined up like standing dominoes. My plan was to climb in between two of the triangles and be whisked off. But to where? Heaven? I don't know.

When I awoke, I was in a hospital bed with my new "baby" beside me, and my throat was as miserable as ever. When the ice cream started arriving, I magically felt better, but for many years after, I couldn't drink from a water fountain without the water coming back out my nose, and once, while I was eating popcorn, a corn kernel did the same.

During our year or so in Appleton, I saw my first movies. I believe the first was *Snow White,* but *The Song of Bernadette,* which I saw around the same time, remains much clearer in my mind. Mom took Grandma and me to see *Bernadette,* the story of the little French girl who saw a vision of the Virgin Mary. When that beautiful, ghostly lady appeared, I disappeared. I tore out to the lobby and sat there until Mom came to see what was wrong. She promised to come get me when the vision sequence finished, and so she did. However, soon there was Mother Mary, back in the grotto, and out I fled again. I suppose Mom and I continued our hide and seek game throughout the entire film. Grandma, who was Orange Irish (Protestant), wasn't thrilled with me, Bernadette, *or* the Blessed Apparition. Grandma was not fond of Catholics, period, so I've often wondered why she came to that particular movie. It's amusing how many of her children and grandchildren married into the Catholic faith. At least, it's amusing to me.

Another first for me in Appleton was "swimming" at the Mill Pond. At the far end of the pond was a small cement bath house for changing clothes. Local kids spent hours cavorting in the pond, and after I ascertained that there were no bloodsuckers there, I would don my bathing suit and cavort along with the best of them. One day I entered the dressing room to change back into my dress before going home, and to my utter disgust, somebody had taken my nice pink underpants and left a dirty gray pair in their place. Rather than wear them, I marched home *au naturel* beneath my skirt.

Mom finally decided she couldn't work at Penney's, keep an eye on Dad, who was still quite sick, and watch every move I made. Since working was a necessity, and a sick husband took priority, I found myself with more freedom than I'd ever enjoyed before. After all, I was six years old, and in the first grade, and didn't need a Hovercraft any more. She had to rely on her old tactic of scaring the spit out of me, hoping that would make me a careful and cautious child. There had been a terrible murder that summer. Somewhere in this huge land of ours, a little six-year-old girl was killed and dismembered. Pieces of the body were found over a period of time and the gruesome story was reported on the news for weeks. Mom took this as a sure sign that she was justified in suspecting a felon lurked behind every bush, waiting to pounce. She warned me over and over what could happen if I talked to strangers or ventured too far from the nest.

I'm still here, so perhaps her strategy had merit. I was a pretty cautious kid, sometimes even a "chicken-livered little scaredy-cat," according to some of my more adventurous pals. I eventually used the same scare tactics on my own girls, and they didn't come to any serious harm while on my watch either, so I guess you can't argue with success.

We learned that one can't protect a child from everything, all the time, though.

During my exciting sixth year, I'd become friends with a little girl whose family owned a gas station in downtown Appleton. Her granddad would let us come and play in some of the old cars around the place. One day, when no other adults were around, Gramps called me over to the shop, took me on his knee and began to "play doctor." When he tried to remove my underpants, I yanked away and ran for my life and my virtue, straight to Mom at Penney's, where I complained bitterly about such disgusting treatment.

Mom never doubted me for a minute, but took me straight to the police station and reported the incident. Apparently she didn't file charges but only told the policeman to keep an eye on the old bugger. Today we would certainly press charges, but in that time and place, Mom didn't think it was the right thing to do.

Dad was still too sick to work. To add to his miseries, he had to have all his teeth extracted. I was with him the day he had them all pulled and the new choppers set in place, and I cried when I saw the results, for I thought they made him look very big-bad-wolfish. The dentist took my reaction personally and gave me a royal scolding, which I've never forgotten. It's best not to comment on a person's appearance (or work) if you can't say something positive.

I had mixed feelings about that dentist. He amazed his young patients with a wonderful trick, involving putting a drop of "magic medicine" on his thumb, and then lifting the thumb right off his hand. He was very good at it, and I was a gullible believer. However, he agreed with my parents that I must have the membranous cord which ran between my two front teeth removed. This "condition" was inherited from my mother, whose two front teeth were somewhat separated and who had definite ideas about how her little girl's teeth were going to line up. I didn't have a chance. Snip, snip, stitch, stitch, all gone. But whatever misgivings I had were misplaced. My adult teeth grew in quite straight, and aside from a slight overbite, I doubt I would have needed braces even if they had been available to me.

My dad's oldest sister, Aunt Lillian, came to visit that year, and, to demonstrate to a little girl what would happen if she neglected her dental hygiene, maneuvered her tongue in such a manner that she could flip her false teeth out like a snake's tongue. She made her point to the extent that ever since, I've brushed and flossed much longer and rougher than my dentist says is necessary.

During our year in Appleton I learned another sort of lesson. This one involved a newly hatched baby robin that I was delighted to find in a nest in our yard. Dad told me to stay away from it or I'd scare the mother away, and then the little peeper would die of starvation. I just couldn't leave it alone. Sure enough, the mama bird abandoned it. Its pitiful cries made me sick, and I knew it was all my fault. Finally Dad told me that I would be doing it a kindness if I put it out of its misery quickly. I begged him to do it, but he said it was my responsibility. I sat on the front stoop and cried and thought long and hard about what I'd done, and how I could kill that homely, naked little bird as painlessly (to both of us) as possible. The garden hoe was my sad weapon of choice.

The bird died quickly, and I learned to take responsibility and make restitution when my actions cause pain. Killing the bird may not technically be "restitution," but I do believe it was better than letting it slowly starve. I suffered so over that little robin that I never wanted to hurt another living thing (with the possible exception of mice and bugs that invade my home).

Was Dad too harsh? I don't think so. Stubborn, willful children sometimes need harsh lessons for their own good and the good of society in general.

During the summer after first grade, Dad grew more certain that he was dying of cancer. He insisted that if he had to die, he was going to do it in Alaska. No amount of reasoning persuaded him otherwise. We sold our little house, bought a maroon International pickup and headed west toward Seattle to catch the first available boat to Seward.

The war had ended, and the Alaska Steamship Company was running regular weekly ships, so my folks felt sure we would be able to board within a few days of arrival in Seattle. Then, somewhere on a long, dusty road in Montana, we heard on the radio that Alaska Steamship Company workers had gone on strike.

At their offices down on the Seattle docks, Alaska Steam officials told us they had no idea how long the strike would continue. We were stranded, and in pretty sad shape. Mom found an "auto court," the forerunner of our present motels, where we could rent a room with cooking facilities. Located a considerable distance from downtown Seattle, at the far end of Boeing Field, this room became home for the next five months, with the three of us sharing a double bed.

I started second grade, Dad took to the bed, miserably weak and sick, and Mom found a job in a Manning Coffee Shop downtown. Every night when we went to bed, I'd crawl in with my head at their feet and pray fervently that Dad wouldn't die—or more specifically, that he wouldn't die while I was in bed with him.

That must have been a terrible time for Mom, yet I never heard her complain about it. She must have been extremely worried about Dad and our future in Alaska, if we ever got back. Whether he lived or died, our prospects were less than zero. And of course, she was always fearful that something awful would happen to me without her watchful attention.

She doubled her warnings. I was NOT to wander away from our unit when I got home from school. I was absolutely NOT to talk to strangers. I was to be in our room before darkfall in the evening. "Yeah, yeah, OK, Mama."

Late one afternoon I skipped up to the gas station/grocery store in front of the auto court to chat with the folks who ran the business. Despite Mom's admonitions, I'd become quite chummy with them, and fortunately, they were kind, good people who didn't seem to mind a lonely little girl hanging around.

I visited a bit beyond my normal stay. Before I knew it, daylight had flown, and the cars whizzing by on the highway had their headlights on. I thought I still had time to beat Mom home, so I wasn't overly concerned as I waved goodbye and set off down the long line of detached cabins with carports dividing them. Horse-chestnut trees heightened the darkness, as I skipped along, cheerily singing "Mairzy Doats" and "Three Ittie Fitties in an Ittie Bittie Poo" at the top of my lungs.

"Now I gotcha!" roared a dark figure as it pounced at me from

Second-grader Arlene, Seattle

behind a parked car. I must have jumped a foot straight up in the air. I still remember squeaking, "Yipes!" as I hit the road running as fast as my trembling legs would carry me. Nearly breaking the door down, I tumbled into our room and into bed with Dad, burrowing beneath the covers. Before I could compose myself enough to tell the tale, Mom appeared at the door. I learned much later that she'd taken a minute or two to stop laughing. By the time she arrived, she was looking pretty serious. "See how easy it is to grab a little girl?" she queried pointedly.

I don't remember a single thing about my first few months in second grade. We still have the report cards, but school in Seattle is a total blank. I can't recall how I got to school, or any friends or teachers. I do remember making frequent trips with my folks on weekends down to the docks to see how the strike was coming along. (Very nicely, I guess.) I recall Dad lifting me up on a piling on the pier that stretched far out over the water, and us singing, "We're Sailing Home," a Sunday School song. The song is actually about dying and going to Heaven, but I thought it was about going home to Alaska. Dad kept his own counsel, but I imagine he was interpreting it both ways.

A couple of times we walked up to the Bon Marche and gazed into their windows at the marvelous mechanical Christmas displays— Santa's workshop, carolers, the nativity scene, with Mary bending to gently touch the Christ Child's head. They were absolute magic; we were all three enthralled.

Finally, the week before Christmas, the strike ended. I had no idea whether the workers or management came out ahead. I didn't care. We were sailing home.

7

EXCEPT WE DIDN'T HAVE A HOME any more. My folks had sold our little cabin across from Doc's store to Bill Brattain and his family. We arrived in Hope the day before Christmas, and Mom and Dad were much relieved to find and rent an empty cabin belonging to an old-timer named Tom Sobol.

This aged log cabin consisted of two rooms, a kitchen in front and a bedroom/living room to the rear. In the latter were a double bed, a small cot, two chairs, a table and a Franklin stove. Mom made up the beds and we fell exhausted into them. The Dragline Kid was back on familiar ground.

On Christmas morning Mom spoke across the darkened room to me: "Honey, look at the stove and see if the fire's still going." I raised myself on one elbow and peered sleepily in that general direction.

There, lighted by the glow from the little triangular windows in the front of the stove, leaning on a shiny chrome kickstand, was a beautiful brand-new blue Sears Roebuck J.C. Higgins bicycle.

I was stunned. Speechless. So much so that I couldn't trust myself to speak, to admit to anybody how thrilled and touched I was by my parents' unbelievable generosity and love. To think that they had somehow managed to buy that treasure and arrange to have it shipped to Hope and then to set it up in the middle of the night in that gloomy old rented cabin. Knowing how sick Dad was, how tenuous our financial situation had to be, how hard Mom had to work for a pittance—it was as if I had been turned to stone.

After a long moment, I simply said, "Yeah, the fire is going." Nothing more. Doesn't that beat all? Tears burn my eyes every time I think of my graceless behavior. Wicked, ungrateful little wretch that I might have seemed to those dear parents who had given me such a gift. But somehow they understood. I just needed a minute to compose myself, or I would have flown into a million little pieces.

In the next heartbeat I was out of that cot, across the ice-cold linoleum, hugging my folks as tight as only a hysterical seven-year-old can hug.

I was crazy about that bike. It's the only one I ever owned. It was enough. Because it was adult-sized, it was too large for me at first, but I insisted I could handle it. I struggled and fought it, I fell on it and it fell on me. At one point I rode it into a ditch at the side of the road and did permanent damage to a very tender and private part of my female anatomy. I didn't worry about myself but fussed over that bike as if it were a living creature. I learned to ride it as if it were a continuation of my own body, zipping all over town without once touching the handlebars.

Because I found such joy in my bike, I wanted Mom to learn to ride it, too. She'd never ridden a bicycle and said she was much too old to learn, but she finally agreed to give it a whirl. Although she was quite a bit bigger than I, I tried my best to steady her as she tried her best to balance. We were off, but not running. We staggered, we teetered, we flopped from one side of the road to the other. And we laughed so hard at our own ineptness that Mom threatened to wet her knickers. Abandoning the bicycle lesson, she made a mad dash for the privy, and by mutual consent we never tried that again.

Although Dad still didn't feel very well, he did start to improve. There was no work for him in Hope, but we settled in for the winter anyway. We had no place else to go. I finished the second grade in the little one-room schoolhouse. Along the way, of course, there were a few adventures.

In February we planned a Valentine's Day program at school, to which the entire town was invited. Leslie Brattain, the roly-poly, rosy-cheeked son of the man who had bought our old cabin, was a year or two older than I, but we were teamed up to sing a duet: "Let Me Call You Sweetheart." Each day for a week, Leslie waded through the snow to our place to practice. Mom was our singing coach and insisted not only on proper enunciation and pitch, but also that we use appropriate facial expressions and body language. Leslie was a very good sport. He suffered my snuggling and cow-eyed adoration without complaint, and I thought he was a perfect "Sweetheart."

Two days before the program, a bunch of us went sledding over at Millers' place. We doubled up, one kid lying on top of the other, for a more challenging ride. With my usual luck and dexterity, while taking the "top bunk" I fell off the sled, which the other kid was piloting, and the sled and the kid ran right over my face. Almost

Gene Boe, holding Pat Brattain, with Shirley Boe and Leslie Brattain

Leslie Brattain

immediately my right eye puffed up and started to turn black and blue. By the evening of the program, I had a shiner that would make Rocky Balboa look like Miss America. I was devastated, but the show must go on. Leslie looked a little strained as he grabbed my hand and hauled me onto the stage. But to his eternal credit, he looked me straight in the eye (the good eye) and sang, "Let me call you sweetheart, I'm in love with you. Let me hear you whisper that you love me, too. Keep the lovelight glowing in your eyes so blue . . ." and never so much as cracked a smile. Everybody else in town had a good laugh, but Leslie was a compassionate boy.

That winter Mom knitted me a pair of bright red mittens. Apparently the dye hadn't "set," because every time I wore them, my hands turned scarlet. Mom and I went to visit Mrs. Brenner one frosty day, and while the women chatted in the kitchen, I played in the yard with Mrs. B's dog. The animal must have read the same book as Peggy Nutter's cow, because he suddenly flung himself onto my leg and began humping away. I assumed he was hugging me, and yelled for Mom to come and see. When she and Mrs. Brenner came out on the porch they got the giggles, and I finally caught on. I gave the dog a kick, disengaging him from my mortified leg, and ran to hide in the woodshed. They soon found me and coaxed me out with cookies, but when I took my mittens off, I heard Mrs. Brenner snicker, "Look, she's so embarrassed even her hands are blushing."

At the height of Alaskan winters, sunlight is a rare and wonderful treat. The sun comes up in the morning, but instead of traveling across the sky from east to west, it almost immediately falls like a stone, gone from sight until the next day's brief peep show. Out of doors, we carried flashlights any hour of the day or night. A person would as soon leave home without his pants as without his flashlight. Some nights, though, it almost seemed daylight, when the full moon shining on the snow cast a beautiful light so bright we could see our shadows.

Inside, cabins were lit by kerosene or gas lamps. We had one with a gizmo on the side that needed frequent pumping to keep the light going. If it didn't receive prompt attention, it gradually dimmed until we realized we were bumping into each other, and somebody went and pumped the lamp up again.

One night I was reading a particularly engrossing Nancy Drew mystery, standing at the table where the lamplight was brightest. As the light imperceptibly grew dimmer, I unconsciously drew closer. All of a sudden Mom gave a shriek, leapt across the room and started whacking me about the head and shoulders with her magazine. Stunned, I thought for sure she'd gone "just like Ivy," but she was saving my life. The top of my head had come in contact with the lamp and burst into flame. Except for some singed curls and a near heart attack, there was no harm done.

Believe it or not, this happened to me again many years later. While I was standing in line for a ride at Disneyland with my family, the young man behind me suddenly started hitting me on the head and back. He'd lit a cigarette and accidentally caught my hair on fire.

Much worse than my own run-in with fire was the day a forest fire broke out several miles from Hope. As soon as we heard about it, the men grabbed their shovels, axes, gunny sacks, buckets, pails and anything else that might be useful, and set off to fight the blaze, while the women and children stood wringing their hands and praying. We didn't wring and pray very long, though. The women mobilized into teams of sandwich-builders and coffee-makers, and in no time a bunch of us loaded the food into our pickup while others stayed to prepare additional victuals.

As we neared the fire, the air grew heavy with smoke and ash. We stopped at a clearing where other vehicles were parked and a few men were conferring. We could see the fire raging on a ridge just off the road; the sound and smell were intense, and so was the heat. Every so often, a man would come stumbling out of the woods and fall wearily to the ground. I didn't even recognize my own father when he came lurching out. All the men were covered with soot and dirt. They resembled the cast of a minstrel show, with only their mouths and eyes unblackened.

I don't remember how long the fire blazed, or how it was extinguished. But I know the Lord was with our men, for not one of them was injured seriously, and not a great deal of timber was lost either. Everybody felt pretty grateful, proud of themselves and each other when it was all over.

Another fire experience was really a very tiny little fire: more of a glowing ember, actually. Shirley Boe and I still played together every possible minute and were always looking for new adventures. If we happened to be hanging around when her dad, Homer, ran out of smokes, he'd say, "How about you girls running over to Doc's an' buy me some Camels?" He'd toss us a quarter, or whatever a pack of cigarettes cost in those days, and off we'd go.

There came a day when we didn't have anything particular with which to amuse ourselves (not infrequent in Hope), and it suddenly came into our heads to take up smoking. I say "our heads" because I don't remember whose bright idea it was, and it would be a cheap shot to blame Shirley when she isn't here to defend herself.

We shook a few coins out of our piggy banks and trotted over to Doc's. The coins were presented and the soft white and gold package was in our hands before you could say, "I'd walk a mile for a Camel." A book of matches was part of the deal.

The Hatch family had moved away, leaving their house and barn empty. The house was boarded up, but the barn offered an excellent retreat. Shirley and I nestled down into the hay and casually lit up. At first we had a little trouble keeping the cigarettes going, but we eventually got the hang of the puff and blow method. I'm quite sure we didn't inhale, or we would have stopped immediately. Instead we huffed and puffed and somehow managed to smoke up the better part of the pack without setting the barn or ourselves on fire. When we decided we'd had enough nicotine rush for the day, we threw what was left of the pack down the Hatches' toilet hole and set about on our next adventure.

Since we were in such a devil-may-care mood, we sidled on down to the flats where a mysterious boat was moored. This boat didn't belong to anybody from Hope and was rarely seen on our mudflats. We knew it belonged to a suspicious-acting fellow from Seward, but nobody knew what his occasional business in Hope might be. There was speculation that he had something to do with bootlegging. At any rate, we had both been told in no uncertain terms to stay away from that fellow AND his boat.

But, after determining that nobody was around, the devil-may-care girls climbed aboard. We were making a furtive examination of the premises when I glanced up and saw a terrifying figure approaching across the flats. Was it the mysterious stranger? Worse. Much worse. It was my mother.

I don't know how she knew where we were. How do mothers know these things? I acquired the same talent when I became a mother and can only assume it's a gift from God. Mom ordered us off the boat, sniffed at our smoke-reeking clothes, eyed our singed eyelashes, and marched us home where she gave me the worst lickin' of my life. Oh, first she heard my side of the story, which was pretty incriminating, and then she gave me a lecture—but then I got a good whopping with the dreaded spank stick.

I wish I could say I learned my lesson and never again touched cigarettes. Unfortunately, years later I took up the nasty habit, and many years after that, I suffered the agonies of the damned when I quit, twice.

Apparently Mom's usual method of locating me hadn't worked. Whenever she wanted me to come home, my mother simply stepped outside our cabin door, lifted both hands to her mouth and yodeled "Ar-leeeeeeeeeeee-ene" in three notes: roughly, C-sharp, G-sharp and F. You could hear her from any point in Hope, except, apparently, out on the mudflats. Her summons echoed off the mountains and vibrated on my humiliated eardrums. The other kids aped her and teased me, and I grew to really hate my name. The fact that Arlene rhymes with stringbean didn't help, either.

When Shirley and I were finally allowed to resume our adventures, we saw a ghost. Yes! We'd moseyed over toward Mr. Beiswanger's place. Beez, one of the old sourdough miners, had died the year before, so his cabin was empty. However, as we approached, we saw in the window the top of Beez's old parchment-colored bald head. We could see it move back and forth as he rocked in his rocking chair. I can still feel the chill that ran down my spine as the tiny hairs on the nape of my neck stood at attention.

Shirley and I took off running like a couple of spooked mice, arriving at my place too breathless to squeak. Mom got us calmed down enough to gasp out our ghostly tale. She flat out didn't believe us. Oh, she knew we were sincere, and that we believed we'd seen a ghost, but *she* didn't believe we had. Finally, rather than argue or reason with us further, she took us both by the hand and marched back over to Beez's.

Shirley Boe and Arlene in Hope

Hope, Alaska Social Hall 1943–44

Hope, Alaska 1940's Community Social Hall

Back row, from left: Teacher Ben Frampton, Joan Witt (Nutter), woman in white (name unknown), Beverly Sobrowsky, woman in dark skirt (name unknown), Mrs. Frampton (in white) with toddler son Clayton, Nellie Brattain, Joe Sobrowsky; two women, in dark jacket and striped shirt (names unknown); Dennie McCart (in hat), seven people with names unknown (Ross Miller behind that group, left of second pillar, face partly obscured), Carl Clark (in back, fifth from right), Homer Boe (white shirt), unknown man looking over from back, old-timer Sam Gates, Harold Davis (side view).

Front row, from left: Bea Davis, May (or Mae) Turpin, unknown small girl, Leslie Brattain (seated in front), Gene Boe (in overalls), Erma Ann Miller (behind Gene), Janice Frampton (with hair bow, next to Erma Ann), Lewie Miller (next to Gene), Patsy Frampton (in white, next to Lewie), unknown girl in white sitting sideways, Donna Turpin (tiny girl in dark clothes), Alice Mitchell, Augustine Boe, Shirley Boe. The Rheingans family was in Minnesota when this photo was taken.

The closer we got, the more Shirley and I dragged our heels. But we had to prove to My Mother The Skeptic that we'd seen a bona fide ghost, so we reluctantly inched closer. And there it was! Just as before, we could see the top of that old yellowish pate right there at the windowsill. And it was still swaying.

Mom burst out laughing. When she could finally speak, she dragged us up to the window and showed us our "ghost": the back of a large, round, yellow clock sitting on the window sill. But how did it move? It didn't. Tall fireweed, swaying in the breeze, were reflected in the window pane, causing the illusion of movement. Shirl and I didn't know whether to be relieved or disappointed. A little of each, I think.

Maybe Mom thought I needed more religion, or maybe she felt I had too much time on my hands. Possibly she just wanted to have a week's peace and quiet. Whatever her motives, she signed me up for Bible Camp.

This may sound like a real treat, and maybe to some kids it is. To me it was exile in Siberia. It was a reluctant seven-year-old who climbed into the two-passenger Piper Cub at our tiny graveled airstrip and flew above the mountains, across the Arm to Anchorage. I'd never been in a plane before, and I was scared to breathe, much less move, for fear I'd rock the boat. Each time the wings dipped, I was sure we were going down. I finally drummed up enough courage to peek out the window at the mountains below and was amazed to see a large bird's nest. It wasn't until a few more flights, and many years later, that I realized I hadn't seen a nest at all, but rather, huge tree trunks, devoid of limbs and leaves, lying higgledy-piggledy at the end of some long-ago avalanche. From our height, it looked exactly like an eagle's nest.

When we landed in Anchorage, someone picked me up at the airport and transported me to the Church of the Open Door, where I joined about 50 other campers. I didn't know anybody. Our suitcases and sleeping bags were tossed into a station wagon, we kids were packed into several rickety old school buses and a few autos, and our little caravan set off for Victory Bible Camp, somewhere in the Matanuska Valley around Palmer.

The camp was brand new. Only one building was actually in existence: the cook shack/mess hall. Our "quarters" were tents on rough wooden floors, about half a dozen kids to each tent, along with an adult counselor. My counselor was a huge woman whose heart was as big as her body. I found that out when it was discovered that my suitcase and sleeping bag had been left behind at the church. She loaned me one of her oversized flannel nightgowns to wear to bed that night. I climbed into the gown and she proceeded to wrap it round and round my little body until I was swaddled like the baby Jesus, or King Tut. Then she picked me up, stiff as a board, and laid me out on my army cot and covered me with a spare blanket.

The next day someone brought my suitcase and sleeping bag, and I at least had clothes to wear for the remainder of the week. The sleeping bag, however, was still a problem. For some reason my mom had rolled up only the sleeping bag cover. I slept in that skimpy little cover, still swathed in the big lady's gown and covered over with various blankets, afghans and mats that people donated throughout the week.

Many of the campers were Native kids from the Lazy Mountain Children's Home who accepted my unorthodox sleeping arrangement with apparent empathy, but there were a few Anchorage snobs who gave me a hard time about it.

I didn't enjoy camp. Not only was I cold at night, but the place was, after all, a tent town, and there were mud and pine needles everywhere. I was used to my mother's warm, clean cabin, and to her tender ministrations. I hadn't realized I'd actually miss her fussing, but I did. And I didn't like having to queue up and sing "Here We Stand Like Birds in the Wilderness" before each meal.

I also didn't like having to "swim" in glacier-fed Victory Lake, or the really vicious mosquitoes, or having to wear a huge wooden dog-tag on a string around my neck for "identification purposes." One person at camp did captivate me, a little Native orphan girl who reportedly had been left as an infant to die in the snow and had, consequently, lost all her toes. We became good friends, and I was fascinated by her stubby little brown feet, about which she was not the slightest bit self-conscious. I sincerely wanted to adopt her.

You'd think that when my mother heard my tales of woe, she would take pity and never force me to go back to Bible Camp. You had better think again. I went for four years running, and while I must admit it got better each year, I never really learned to appreciate the joys of camping.

Back in Hope, I was somewhat of a celebrity, as none of the other kids had ever been to camp. Naturally, I told them only the "fun stuff" and did my sniveling in the privacy of my mother's bosom. My celebrity didn't last long, though, for soon we were all stars of an exciting drama.

Bob Mathison, with whom my folks had mined and trapped eight and nine years earlier, still ran his scow back and forth across the Arm to Anchorage. One spring day when he must have felt particularly brave, he issued a blanket invitation to all the kids in town: a half-day cruise out to Gull Rock. We jumped at the chance. Several of the mothers (for once, not including mine) came along to insure that we behaved ourselves and didn't drive Bob, a long-time bachelor, out of his mind.

We had a beautiful day for the trip. Cruising right up to Gull Rock—actually a series of huge rocks sticking out of the water—we were able to observe the big white seagulls as they swooped and soared above their nests. The nests contained both eggs and baby chicks, and we teased to get as near as possible so we could hear their plaintive cries for food. Bob wanted to make us happy, so he steered the scow in as close to the rocks as he could. Unfortunately, his navigation was off ever so slightly. Suddenly there was a terrific crash, and we came to an abrupt and absolute stop. Those who weren't hanging on fell to the deck.

We'd run into the pointed top of a huge submerged rock, and there we stuck tight.

The tide was going out, fast. Turnagain Arm tides are famous for rapid ebbing and flowing. They are the second-highest tides in the world, and roar in and out with unbelievable speed. Before we knew it, we were high and dry, our scow perched on that rock for all the world like Noah's ark atop Mt. Ararat. Soon the water had completely gone and we were able to walk on the rocks right up onto Gull Rock itself. We were mighty cautious there, because the rocks were slimy and slippery, and the gulls were not happy to have their nesting place visited by a dozen excited, shipwrecked kids. While they shrieked and dove at us, we covered our heads with our coats and then retreated to the relative safety of our teetering vessel.

Someone in town must have been looking through binoculars (my money is on Aunt Emma up on her hill), because shortly after the

Bob Mathison's boat hung up on Gull Rock, 1946 (Arlene on railing, far left)

water rushed out from under us, a group of fathers (mine included this time) formed a rescue party. In hip boots, they came sloshing across two miles of mudflats and carried us piggy-back home to Hope. I felt important and precious as I rode, my legs clasped around my father's broad waist.

I was halfway through my third year of school when my folks gave up Hope. Literally. They knew we couldn't survive there with absolutely no work for either of them.

A road had recently been built to the village of Kenai, south and west on the Kenai Peninsula, where, it was rumored, there might be an opportunity for a job. After a hurried trip to scout out the territory and meet some of the Kenai folk, my parents loaded our few possessions on the back of the pickup, and the three of us said goodbye to Hope.

I left with mixed emotions, as, I suppose, did my parents. On the one hand, I hated to leave my little clique of friends. On the other, I was excited about moving to a "big town."

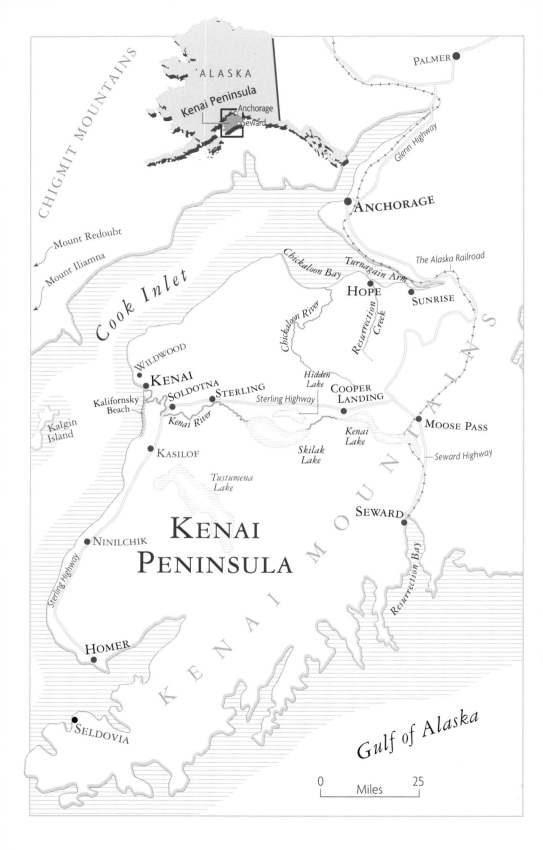

Kenai

8

THE VILLAGE OF KENAI HELD around 300 people when we arrived in the spring of 1948. Located on the upper west side of the Kenai Peninsula, Kenai is situated on an 80-foot bluff at the mouth of the Kenai River, renowned for its record king salmon. Where it meets the village, the river flows into Cook Inlet, an expanse of water that reaches 40 miles across to the "Valley of 10,000 Smokes" in the Chigmit Mountains of the vast Alaska Range. From Kenai, towering Iliamna and Redoubt can be seen looming above all the other peaks across the inlet. Every few years one of the mountains erupts, sometimes sending blankets of ash to cover Kenai. Many years ago, one of the "biggies" erupted and blew boulders the size of small cabins clear across the inlet. Two of them landed on the beach directly below what became our home.

Kenai itself is not surrounded by mountains, as are Hope and Seward. The river and the inlet are its main scenic attributes. The forests around town are cottonwood, birch and scrub spruce. The village had more frame houses than Hope, with its log cabins, but the oldest homes in Kenai are also of weathered gray logs.

Dirt and gravel roads meandered through town, and there was little delineation of where one person's property ended and another's began. For the most part, houses were apparently built wherever the mood happened to strike. There were a few exceptions, carefully marked by fences.

Only a very few homes in town had electricity, which was powered by privately owned generators. For many years nobody had a telephone. My folks never owned one while I lived at home. Almost without exception, everyone had outhouses instead of bathrooms, and water was hand-pumped, from an old iron pump either in the kitchen or out in the yard. Some people still had wells with buckets swinging from ropes.

Electricity came to Kenai around 1950, when Frank Rowley installed a power plant and most of us happily plugged in. Service was erratic at best, but to us it was a miracle.

When we arrived in Kenai, we were the fifth all-white family living in town. Most people's derivations were various combinations of Alaska Native and Scandinavian, Russian, or Filipino. There were other white families living on homesteads scattered throughout the area, and at two government camps a few miles out of town. The Civil Aeronautics Administration (CAA, as everybody called it) had maybe five families in its compound; the Alaska Road Commission (ARC) had another half-dozen.

Kenai family names were foreign and odd to me at first. Those who had Russians perched in their family trees had colorful names like Backoff, Ivanoff, Sacaloff and Mamaloff, while Filipino families were named Segura and Cabanos. Those whose parents or grandparents came from Norway, Sweden, or Denmark might be named Petterson or Juliussen.

Many first names were strange to my ear, too: Ephim, Odman, Posto, Sergay, Ponto and Pilka were some of the men. Women were Agrafena, Nadia, Karitina, Fiocla. Nicknames were colorful, too: Moosemeat John and Half-a-Box spring to mind.

The children of my generation had more familiar first names: Evelyn, George, Carl, Albert, Charlotte, etc.

Everyone spoke English, but a few Russian words popped up now and then: banya for sweathouse, calidor for entrance shed, and the always popular cusswords, of course. Kenai folk had a particular inflection to their speech, one I seem to have picked up immediately. I can't describe it, but strangers still comment on my accent, wondering where I'm originally from.

In the mid-1940s, in an effort to populate Alaska and stimulate the economy, the U.S. government encouraged GIs who had served in World War II to homestead up to 160 acres of Alaska land, in designated areas. They were required only to build a "habitable" dwelling of unspecified size and live on the land for seven months of one year. Many ex-servicemen and some women veterans, too, moved with their young families to the Kenai area about the time we arrived. After they selected their homesteads, land was opened up to non-veterans, who besides the other requirements had to clear a certain amount of acreage.

One young father who had improved his land in the Soldotna area, 10 miles from Kenai, contracted polio and got around in a wheelchair thereafter. When his potato crop was ready for harvesting, many Kenai folks, men, women and children, pitched in and helped Frank Mullen's family dig their spuds. This was not an isolated instance of the spirit of cooperation and caring that was common in Alaska in those days, as it had been in earlier frontier areas.

The head honcho in Kenai was, indisputably, Marshal Allan L. Petersen, a Teddy Roosevelt kind of man, whose wife, Jettie, was one of four teachers at Kenai Territorial School. They were when we arrived, and remained until their deaths, the most respected people in town. Mr. Petersen helped us find a place to live, two rented rooms in the home of a Native man named Nikolai Kalifornsky. Nick, or Nickoloshka as he was often called, was an elderly gentleman whose daughter and son-in-law ran the office of the bi-weekly airliner, Pacific Northern Airlines. His son, Peter, later co-wrote a book on the Dena'ina language of the Kenaitze people.

Kenai was different from Hope in other ways than its family dwellings. Besides the obvious differences of size and ethnic diversity, I had to get used to some subtler distinctions. Of the 60 or so kids who attended school (grade school and high school in one four-room building), most were related in one way or another. While they fought like wolverines among themselves, they didn't take kindly to anybody giving one of their relatives a hard time. By our high shool years, I pretty much knew who was cousin to whom, but I was never sure enough to get cocky.

Kenai had an active population of winos, poor souls who wandered around town day and night, summer or winter, with bottles of cheap booze clutched to their shivering chests. Among my first memories of Kenai are seeing these people stagger past Nickoloshka's house, collapsed in the weeds that grew everywhere, or urinating against anything that wasn't moving. I was very sorry for them, and as I grew up I became friendly with some. They wouldn't hurt a child, but several of them did mortal damage to each other or to themselves.

One old fellow called Curley, in a fit of DTs, imagined himself to be a chicken and cut his own throat. A woman drank lye by mistake, but lived to tell the story. Several drunks ganged up on one of their buddies and killed him one night, and one of them was sent to prison. He swore to Mom when he got out that he'd been framed.

I made several attempts to return various winos to their homes, but eventually gave up and accepted them as a pathetic part of the landscape. A woman whom I never saw sober (and once saw lurching through the snow in her slip) grew to recognize me as I got older. She staggered up to me while I was on a date one night and implored me to take her to the toilet. I did.

Obviously, low tolerance for liquor was a problem in Kenai. Another scourge was tuberculosis. Many local families had lost loved ones to the disease, and several had family members in the sanitarium in Seward. One of the first friends I made after moving to Kenai was a girl whose mother was dying of TB. She'd been in "the San" but had come home to die. She'd sit at her window and watch us play outside her house, occasionally pecking at the windowpane with her finger.

Mom still had a hard time accepting the fact that she couldn't protect me constantly. Reluctantly, she gave me more freedom to roam as all the other kids in town did, but with many caveats and stipulations. I was allowed to play with any of the kids I wished, but it was understood that I was not to go into certain homes. This rule was relaxed considerably when she became acquainted with individual families, but she still denied me entrance to any homes where TB patients were dying, or where dysfunctional adults were suspected.

Even at the age of eight, I was able to understand her concern and appreciate the reasonableness of her warnings. It didn't take long for me to develop my own sense of right and wrong, safety and risk, and I soon learned to walk that particular tightrope with a certain degree of cautious confidence.

On my very first day of school, Mom walked me over from Nickoloshka's house to the old Kenai Territorial School building, a distance equivalent to about a city block. I joined the other first-, second- and third-graders in Jettie Petersen's classroom, and immediately became the object of scrutiny du jour. My 15 or so classmates appeared neither friendly nor hostile, just curious. Mrs. Petersen was a delightful, grandmotherly lady, the first person I ever knew to grow daffodils in a pot on the windowsill. She must have taught reading, writing and 'rithmetic, but all I remember from those months in her class are the golden daffodils and the song, "Faraway Places": "Faraway places with strange sounding names, far away over the sea —those faraway places, with the strange sounding names, are calling, calling me. . ."

First, second and third graders at teacher Jettie Petersen's house (also the marshal's office and jail): Standing: Sharon Wright, Freda Monfor, Jerry Benson, Sigrid Juliussen, Violet Sanders, Arlene Rheingans; middle row: Larry Sanders, Skip White, Nels Juliussen, Mott Fuller, Tommy—; front: Vince— , Jimmy Segura, Glen Kooly, Billy Ivanoff, Roy Soper, Rudy Wilson

Gertrude Segura and Arlene (top), and Lena Titus

The song goes on to speak of China, and "Siam," and other foreign lands. I don't suppose any of Mrs. Petersen's little people actually expected to see any of those places. I didn't. But in later years I traveled to many of those exotic locations, and on every trip I thought of Mrs. Petersen and that song. I've learned that many of my classmates also became world travelers.

I don't know how it happened in a town as small, sparse, flat and simple as Kenai, but when I set out for home after that first day at school, I got lost. I was crying when a slim, dark, handsome teenage boy came along and, learning we were living at Nick's house, escorted me home. For years I adored Edward Segura, and his little sister, Gertrude, became my first Kenai friend.

That friendship didn't last long, I'm sorry to say. Gert, who was considerably smaller than I, though older and more street smart, soon became my nemesis. Hissing, "I'm gonna beat you up after school," she chilled my heart and kept me in torment for several weeks. Each day after school I'd race for home, positive that Gert was going to clean my clock.

Dad finally wearied of my cowardice. In a rare moment of parental sagacity, he said, "I don't believe in fighting. Not unless you absolutely have to. But the next time Gertrude threatens to beat you up, you just stand your ground, look her straight in the eye and say, 'You go right ahead.' I guarantee she'll back down."

I didn't believe a word he said. I knew if I did that, Gert would make dog-meat out of me. But I was so surprised that Dad had actually taken the initiative to give me some advice that I knew I'd have to follow through. I did, and Dad was right. Gert gulped, "I'll do it tomorrow." But she never mentioned it again. When I saw her nearly 50 years later, she was still petite and cute and feisty, but she wasn't mad at me any more.

Shortly after we arrived in town, an Eskimo family moved into the house next door to Nick's. Their last name was Titus, and they had three or four kids around my age. Lena was several years older than I, but we immediately became close friends. Her brother Jacob was a good pal, too.

The Titus family were the first Eskimos I'd ever seen, and possibly the first to live in Kenai. They were from northwestern Alaska. I realize that generalizations can be dangerous, but I'm going to take that risk and state flat out that I believe the Eskimos to be the most gentle, kind, imaginative, generous and honest people on Earth.

I was charmed by the Tituses. With a stick and a piece of string, those kids could make up games to play all day long. A small log and an old piece of board became a toy we played with for weeks. They taught me to make tiny mukluks from hide or felt, to be decorated with beads and worn as lapel pins. They improvised a version of hopscotch. These were clever, artistic people. Mom approved of our friendship but suggested that I not partake of their food.

It's very difficult—nay, impossible—to refuse an Eskimo's hospitality. Traditionally they become offended if you refuse their gifts. When Grandma Titus invited me to stay for lunch, I tried my darnedest to decline gracefully, but Grandma wasn't having any of that. I knew when I was licked. I ate what was put before me.

Recently I ran across a list of Eskimo words for some of their foods, along with definitions:

> *Mipquq*: Whale meat dipped in seal oil
> *Muktuk*: Whale oil and blubber
> *Quaq*: Frozen fish dipped in seal oil
> *Aqatuq* (also called Eskimo ice cream): Whipped caribou
>   fat oil mixed with sugar, blueberries, blackberries or
>   salmonberries.

It's customary to keep the food around until it is properly "aged." Eskimos have subsisted and thrived on these dishes for centuries. I don't recall what was served that day, but it took a lot of gumption on the part of a little white girl to get whatever it was down. I did, though, and promptly became very ill. I spent several miserable days purging my system from both ends but was soon happily playing with my hospitable friends again. I simply avoided being anywhere near their place when mealtimes rolled around.

We hadn't been living in Kenai long when Dad got a job at Dobinspeck's cannery, one of two fish canneries on the Kenai River. Libby, McNeill & Libby was larger and on the opposite side of the river from Kenai, requiring a boat to get there. Dobinspeck's was only a couple miles upriver from town, just beyond the CAA compound.

Dad was hired as a mechanic and thought he could handle the work, as he was beginning to feel better. It was seasonal, just a summer job, but he was delighted to have it.

He'd been working there only a few weeks when he came home late to dinner one evening with news of considerable excitement at Dobinspeck's. A salty old character named Pappy Walker had been walking through the woods that afternoon with his wife, Jessebelle, and their dog, Boots, from the cannery to their nearby homestead. Suddenly Boots, who had run ahead, began barking fit to kill and then came tearing back with his tail between his legs. Right behind him came two huge Kodiak brown bears. Jessebelle turned and ran back down the trail toward the cannery, but Pappy stepped off the trail and, as the bears ran by, whacked one on the nose with a quart bottle of milk he was carrying.

The bear stopped in its tracks and whacked back—lifted Pappy's scalp right off his skull like you'd peel an orange, flicked one eye out with a long, sharp claw, and pulled Pappy's arm out of the socket. That might have been the end of Pappy, but he had sense enough to play dead, and when the dog came back and began harassing the bears, they lost interest in Pappy.

Heeding Jessebelle's cries, some men from the cannery went down the trail and met Pappy, who incredibly was back on his feet, and hauled him into town. Somebody flew him to Anchorage, where the hospital patched him up and eventually sent him home. Boots was given a medal by the humane society in Anchorage, and Pappy, scarred but irrepressible as before, had another great story to add to his repertoire. He called everybody "Hon," or better yet "Precious," even my father, which I thought was hilarious.

A few years later another homesteader was attacked by brown bears and sustained injuries almost identical to Pappy's. That man also survived. The secret to surviving a bear attack, the experts say, is to play dead as Pappy did. The bear will soon tire of playing with you and wander off. I'd hate to test the theory.

Perhaps Kenai's most outstanding physical feature was "Da Bank." When I first heard kids saying, "I'll meet ya at Da Bank," or "He's playing over at Da Bank," I naturally pictured a financial institution. Something solid, made of bricks and with bars on the windows.

Airfield

Alaska Road Commission

Fish and Wildlife Service

Kenai, Alaska, mid-1950s, looking east

Russian/Native cemetery

Old Russian school

Russian Orthodox church

Nick Kalifornsky's house

The "new" school

Civil Aeronautics Administration

Kenai Joe's roadhouse

The Rheingans' house
and the post office

Kenai River

The Petersens' house
and the jail

Old Kenai Territorial School

Kenai Commercial store

My confusion gave everybody a good laugh, and finally some of the kids walked me over to Da Bank. Of course it's the 80-foot bluff on which Kenai perches, overlooking the river and the inlet.

Da Bank, due to constant erosion, sloughs off a couple feet each year. It's almost perpendicular at the southeast edge of town overlooking the river, but gradually slopes to a more gentle incline toward the southwest, above the flats and the inlet.

The main function of Da Bank, beside holding back the river, more or less, was as the town dump. Everyone who lived along the bluff—my family included, after we bought our own place—made frequent trips to Da Bank to toss over anything they no longer wanted. Those who lived farther away saved up their garbage and dumped it whenever the pile got too high, or when they happened to be near Da Bank. The closer you lived to it, the more you appreciated its convenience.

Over went our daily "slop bucket" (containing all nasty waste except human excrement, which was dumped down the toilet hole); the contents of Dad's spit can, discarded mail, old clothes, furniture that absolutely could not be repaired one more time, dead animals, broken dishes—you get the picture. This community dumping occurred mostly on the southeast side (our side) of the village, where it was hoped the garbage would tumble all the way down the steep cliff onto the beach and eventually be washed away by a high tide.

However, much trash eventually piled up on the more gradual section of the slope, where it remained for years. I shudder to report that this site became a favorite "shopping mall" for us kids. It was our very own second-hand store/antique shop/information center—and the price was always right. By reading discarded letters we acquainted ourselves with the town's secrets. Old magazines, especially *True Detective, Esquire* and *National Geographic,* were prized for their educational value. Especially the pictures. And we'd struggle for days lugging some dilapidated old table or couch up Da Bank to use in our forts and open-air playhouses.

Unsightly, unsanitary, smelly and downright dangerous (one little boy was killed when Da Bank sloughed off and buried him), Da Bank drew us like a magnet. If an old tree clung tenaciously to the bluff's edge, some brave kid would tie a long rope around its upper trunk so we could take turns leaping into space and swinging around to land safely back on terra-not-quite-firma.

Lying on my tummy at the edge of Da Bank on a warm, lazy summer day, I had the best view in the world. Fishing boats ("drifters") moving against the flow of the river to unload their catch at the canneries. Snow-covered volcanoes puffing placidly across the inlet. Beluga and seals frolicking at the mouth of the river. And every so often, somebody heaving his garbage over the bluff. Pure romance.

For the most part, Da Bank smelled just about as bad as you would expect. There was, however, a mysterious exception. In front of the Kenai Bible Chapel, where the bluff began to gentle out somewhat, was a steep, oft-traveled trail going down to the beach. One day as I was panting my way back up, just before the top, there came to my nostrils a most beautiful aroma. It was as fragrant as any perfume, and such a change that I stopped in my tracks and looked around to find the source. There in the side of the bluff was a shallow indentation—not large, maybe 16 inches across and six inches deep. As I stuck my nose closer to this little "cavelet," the aroma increased. Very sweet, and entirely unfamiliar to me. Yes, the smell was positively coming from that spot. Many times I noticed the same fragrance as I climbed Da Bank, and for the life of me, I don't know why I didn't bring a shovel and at least try to uncover the mystery. It's not at all like me to let something of that sort go without a struggle. The last time I was in Kenai, I looked for the spot, but that section of Da Bank had long since broken off and fallen into the inlet.

We had rented from Nick only a few months when something happened that enabled my folks to buy the old log cabin we moved into at the southeast end of town, right on Da Bank.

The cabin, fairly good-sized, was set back from the bluff some 150 feet, giving us a large yard, fenced with chicken wire. And it was beach-front property, albeit the beach was 80 or 90 feet below, straight down. Each year we lost a foot or two to erosion, but Mom and Dad figured we'd be long dead before it ate its way back to the house. (When I went back for a visit 40 years after I left Kenai, Da Bank had progressed to within 50 feet of our front door, and now the beautiful house my dad built to replace the old cabin is in imminent danger of tumbling into the river, too.)

The Rheingans' first home in Kenai

The boon that enabled us to purchase our own place was misfortune for somebody else. One day the postmaster, a middle-aged lady I'll call "Mrs. W.," lost her mind. She had, apparently, been T.F.N.T.L., the Alaskan's abbreviation for Too Far North Too Long. A mild form of this is called simply "cabin fever," but that, while not exactly fun, is not certifiable. T.F.N.T.L. *is* certifiable, and when Mrs. W. lost her mind, locked the stamps and money orders in the safe and went tearing down the main street of Kenai, dropping off garments as she ran, Marshal Petersen apparently had no recourse but to ship her out to Morningside Hospital.

Kenai needed another postmaster. According to Civil Service regulations, the postmaster was required to have at least a high school diploma, which narrowed the field considerably. When word went out, my mother and two other people applied for the job. Marshal Petersen asked Mom to run the office on a temporary basis, and when he saw what a good job she was doing, he endorsed her for the permanent position. She took the tests, and a year later, the Postmaster General under President Truman officially appointed her the Kenai postmaster.

Our ship had come in. We were headed uptown, if there had been an uptown in Kenai. We bought the 50-year-old cabin on Da Bank, and Dad was feeling well enough to buy a fish site across the river a few miles up Kalifornsky Beach. He had a tiny frame cabin there, and for several years he'd live there during the summer months and set his nets to catch the salmon headed toward the Kenai River. He seemed to thrive with just his Zenith short-wave radio for company. Each summer Mom and I thought maybe he'd break down and write us a letter, and finally one day we got a note via Libby's mail carrier. Written carefully in pencil it read: "Send me the stuff that makes my teeth stay in."

By then my mother was running the P.O. out of a shed attached to our cabin and had been authorized to hire her friend Ruth Grueninger as her assistant. Mom was pretty preoccupied with her new position and responsibilities and probably didn't really mind being deserted. Dad, as I've said before, was never very talkative anyway. (As they were leaving Alaska permanently after 25 years in the Land of the Midnight Sun, Dad mentioned how much he had enjoyed living there. "I loved every minute of it," he said. "How about you?" Mom was silent. She finally admitted that no, she hadn't loved every minute of it—that at times she was ready to jump up and down and holler. "In fact," she confessed, "until I got the post office I was really very unhappy with our poor lot in life." Dad was dumbfounded. "Why, I never knew you felt that way!" he exclaimed. I find this exchange either a demonstration of Dad's complete lack of observation or a testament to Mom's eternally accommodating good nature. Or a combination of the two. At any rate, it exemplifies their relationship.)

Sometimes I helped out in the post office, hand-canceling outgoing letters and sorting incoming mail. I became quite adept at sneaking magazines out of their mailing sleeves, reading them surreptitiously, and then twisting them carefully back into their brown paper wrappers. Thus I read *Life, Look, Saturday Evening Post* and various movie magazines, and my knowledge of the outside world was considerably enhanced, though somewhat skewed.

Our new home had a main floor and a roomy, tall attic that we never used except for storage. The floors in the cabin were uneven, covered with well-worn linoleum. We had a kitchen, a front room, a bedroom, and a tiny second bedroom, just large enough to accommodate a small dresser and a twin bed. The dresser crowded up against the foot of the bed, so the bottom two drawers could never be opened. This was my bedroom. I had an even tinier closet, in which I hung my clothes and where our chamber pot dwelt. On cold winter nights, when a person couldn't abide wading through the snow to the outhouse, that person would come quietly into my room, remove the pot from my closet, face into the closet, and do his or her duty.

My room never smelled like a rose, but one time it got really obnoxious. Mom and I hunted out the source and found it in a Mason jar under my bed. I had collected some small white shells on the beach and put them in the jar for safekeeping. Sadly, all the shells weren't unoccupied; many of them still had little creatures living in them until I innocently signed their death warrants. They had their revenge, though. In those days we didn't have air fresheners, and I lived with their "ghosts" for a long time.

Twice in childhood I walked in my sleep. The first time we were still living in Hope. Mom found me in the kitchen, staring at a cabinet, saying, "Where's that sugar bowl?" The second time she found me standing in my little closet in Kenai, with one bare foot in the chamber pot.

On one wall of my room was a window that looked into the chicken yard. I kept the shade tightly drawn, as I was scared of spooks and from that window I could also see three graves and hear our rabbits in their hutch, moving around at night and making strange thumping noises.

On the other wall I kept my collection of comic book glamour girls. Katy Keene from the Archie comics was my ideal, but I cut out other beautiful cartoon babes and pinned them to my wall with thumb tacks in their navels. I still have all those beauties in a big tattered envelope. When I look at them, I feel like a 10-year-old again.

Our cabin was beastly cold in the winter. We had a wood cooking stove and a wood-burning heater in the front room, but during the night they would burn out, and by morning the teakettle on the kitchen stove would have ice inside. Mom was usually the first one up, so she got the fires going, but it was still hard to leave the warmth of those flannel sheets, and the fluffy down comforter.

Shortly after we moved into our own place, I acquired a little black dog of uncertain parentage, possibly cocker spaniel and Scotty, on a rare trip to Anchorage. Following up on a newspaper ad that read "PUPPIES FOR SALE," I arrived at the seller's home with something like $2 clutched in my fist. Those puppies were the cutest things I'd ever seen, especially the runt, who showed more gumption than all the rest put together.

I was smitten with that pup. When I ventured to ask the price, the man said, "$5," and I felt my heart sink. After a pause he said, "But for the little girl who loves that puppy so much, I'll just have to let him go for nothing."

The pup wasn't housebroken, so my folks said he'd have to ride home to Kenai in the back of the pickup. I feared he'd be cold, so we made a warm bed for him to lie on. Then I fretted that he'd jump out and run away, so Dad tied a rope around his neck and attached it to the truck.

We were tooling along the road approaching Cooper Landing when Dad suddenly grunted softly (his way of expressing extreme agitation), slammed on the brakes and ripped open his door. He raced to the back of the truck, where the rope hung ominously over the tailgate. Mom and I crept behind, fearing to discover a furry little corpse dangling at the end of the rope.

There instead, rolling ass-over-eyebrows, was the pup, who had been dragged who knows how far over the gravel road. He looked pretty scruffy, and a lot annoyed, and the pads of his paws were raw. But he was a long ways from a goner.

I named him Tuffy, and he rode the rest of the way home on my lap. That dog was phenomenal! With coaching from me and Jimmy Petersen, the marshal's son and my dad's best friend who was also assistant refuge manager of the Kenai National Moose Range, Tuffy learned tricks like a circus dog. He could sit up, beg, shake hands, roll over, play dead, catch a morsel off the end of his nose, and just about anything else you can think of.

Besides being a talented entertainer, Tuffy was my constant companion and sleeping partner. Because my room was so cold in the winter, Mom permitted Tuffy to burrow down between the sheets, to the very foot of the bed, where he slept contentedly and apparently without oxygen all night, keeping my feet toasty as can be.

One summer around my 10th year I was allowed to visit Dad for a week at the fish site. His cabin was about 8 x 8 feet, furnished with only a bed, a homemade fold-up table, a camping stove, a Blazo box with a few dishes and some beat-up silverware, a frying pan, one saucepan, the Zenith radio, a round metal dishpan, and Dad's spit can. There was barely room for Dad, let alone me—and of course Tuffy.

I'm not sure how Dad felt about having company, but I like to think he enjoyed us. He was more communicative than I remember him at any other time. Tuffy and I were delighted to be there. I knocked myself out trying to be a good houseguest: peeling potatoes, making the bed, washing dishes, even helping mend nets.

While we were there, the tides ran such that sometimes the nets required "picking" during the night. Since it was summer, it was light all night, so we'd go to bed and sleep until the alarm went off. Then Dad would get up and, in his small dory, go out and pick the nets, pulling them by hand over the bow of the dory. He'd wrestle the salmon free from the net and they'd tumble, slippy-sliding, to the floor of the dory. There usually weren't more than five or six fish, and sometimes even fewer. I begged to go with him, but he was reluctant.

Erv Rheingans at his fish site cabin

Ruth Grueninger and Arlene, picking gooseberries at Hope

Arlene's 10th birthday party at Millers' in Hope: Carla Mae Clark, Erma Ann Miller, Berdie Clark, Arlene, Linda and Lewie Miller

I suppose he was afraid I'd get hurt, or fall out of the boat, or maybe he just didn't want the Kid to get in his way.

About midway through our visit, I finally wore him down. This didn't happen often with my father. However, one night when the alarm went off he said, "OK, get your jacket on. You're going to be a fisherman." Since we slept in our clothes, it didn't take long for me to join him at the water's edge. Tuffy had to content himself with racing back and forth along the beach, furious at being left behind.

We could see Dad's neighbors shoving off in their own dories or already picking their nets. I was a-tingle with excitement. For about two minutes.

Then, as we rocked gently at anchor 250 feet from shore, the surging motion of the waves swaying up and down, up and down, back and forth, back and forth, I quit tingling and began to suspect that I'd made a huge mistake. Maybe I wasn't cut out to be a fisherman. Trying hard to hide my misery, I struggled to maintain my dignity. But when Dad tossed a plug-ugly flounder in my lap and I saw that it had both eyes on the same side of its head, I lost my beans and weinies over the side.

Except for that night, that week was one of the highlights of my childhood. I was so delighted to have my dad's attention, and I wished he'd always be my pal, but he just wasn't that kind of father.

For my 10th birthday, I was invited to return to Hope for a week to visit old friends. I stayed at the Miller home, across the flats from town. Their mother, Alma, was a vivacious woman, full of chat and fun, and I very much enjoyed the kids, Erma Ann, Lewie and little Linda. I'm wondering now why I didn't stay at Shirley Boe's house, but I didn't.

Alma threw a birthday party for me and invited all the kids in town. Despite my disinclination toward parties, this was great fun. Naturally, I had tales to tell about life in the big city and my new Kenai pals. Those little "provincials" listened with wide eyes. I didn't tell them any of the negative things.

The Miller kids and I enjoyed an imaginative correspondence when I returned to Kenai. Sometimes we'd write everything backward, from right to left, which required a mirror to read. Or, we'd write in a spiral, starting our letters in the middle of the page, spiraling round and round in ever larger circles until we reached the edges of the paper and could spiral no more. A few times we used lemon juice and a seagull feather to pen invisible missives, but that required a lot of work: One had to hold the seemingly blank page over a source of heat (a candle, perhaps) in order to bring out the words. This was no doubt a trick learned from those Nancy Drew mysteries of which I was extremely fond.

That correspondence may have been responsible for my everlasting love of writing and receiving letters. In my opinion, letters are far superior to telephone calls, for one can enjoy them many times over. And you can't save a telephone call for posterity.

9

DURING THE WAR, AN AIRSTRIP HAD been hastily hacked out of the woods to the north of Kenai, and the U.S. Army had actually constructed make-believe airplanes with wooden frames and canvas "skins" that they displayed on the runway in apparent hopes that any Japanese passing over would think Kenai had a lean, mean fighting machine. I don't suppose it ever occurred to the U.S. Army that this might also make Kenai a prime target for Japanese attack.

At any rate, the remains of some of those old counterfeit planes were rotting in the woods beside the airfield when I arrived in Kenai. We played in them until they finally disintegrated and became one with the undergrowth.

Since a real airplane landed only six or seven times a week, we felt we had free access to the airstrip for whatever purposes we wished. It was a grand place to ride our bikes. In the winter, when moose wandered into town, someone would often have to shoo them off the cleared runway so the mail plane or the PNA bi-weekly passenger and freight flight could land.

One day while roaming around at the end of the runway, I discovered a cylindrical white cardboard container, about the size of a quart of ice cream. It had a nice snug lid, and I figured that if it didn't contain some treasure, at the very least it would make a handy receptacle for one of my many "collections," i.e. rocks, shells, Sugar Daddy cards, etc.

With some difficulty and much expectation I pried off the lid, only to find that my treasure box was in actuality a used barf-box. As I tossed it back among the weeds, I thought what a shame it was that such an attractive container should go to waste. In my world, we became great scroungers and savers. You couldn't just run to the nearest store and buy whatever you needed. Waste Not, Want Not, said the framed sampler in the kitchen of Mrs. Lewis, a homesteader's wife. That impressed me greatly. Waste became my enemy forevermore.

My dad drove the pickup to Seward twice a year to get case lots of groceries the folks ordered from the Tacoma Packing Company in

Washington state. During these trips, he'd invariably spend some time at the Seward dump, where he'd usually find a "treasure" of his own. Once it was an aged black wooden wall clock. After he tinkered with it, it chimed the hours on our wall for many years. I've seen similar ones in antique shops for shocking prices. Another time he brought home a discarded couch. He and Mom completely disassembled it and rebuilt it from the frame out, and we had a pretty decent couch. But his piece de resistance was an upright piano.

Some guy who owned a bar in Seward had bought a new piano and was just unloading his old, beat-up one when Dad arrived at the dump. After the bar man drove away, Dad pushed the piano onto the pickup and came home very pleased with himself. That piano took some time to repair, but it was a real find.

At the end of the keyboard was a curious lever. Dad attached a long, lightweight board inside the piano to this lever and covered the board with oilcloth cut in saw-tooth V's, each of which had a brass brad attached to its tip. When the lever was flipped, dropping the slat down, the hammers struck the brad while striking the string and the result was a delightful rinky-tink sound. Of course, while playing "Rock of Ages" or "Amazing Grace," one would keep the lever forward, but ripping through "When You Wore a Tulip" or "When Irish Eyes Are Smiling" was all the more satisfying with that lever in the backward position.

Now that we had a piano, I had to take piano lessons again. For a while Jimmy Petersen's wife, Evelyn, taught me. She was a pretty young lady from Fort Collins, Colorado, whom Jimmy had met and married while attending the Colorado School of Agriculture and Mines. I think she was a bit dismayed to find herself in Kenai. The newlyweds lived with Jimmy's parents until the Quonset hut that the Fish and Wildlife Service supplied for housing was available.

For some reason, my lessons were soon transferred to Eldy Covich, the distaff half of a husband and wife missionary team who served the Lord at the Kenai Bible Chapel, a non-denominational mission church supported by the Slavic Gospel Association, headquartered in Chicago. Since the point was to supply missionaries to Russian-speaking people, and 99.9% of Kenai spoke only English, one wonders how they came to be there. However, it was the only church in town at the time besides the picturesque Russian Orthodox Church. During our

*Four generations: Peggy Petersen Arness with Jimmie Allan
Arness, Bertha Stryker, Jettie Stryker Petersen*

Jimmy and Evelyn Petersen

years in Kenai, the Chapel was served by a number of missionary teams.

For years the Kenai Chapel's ministers and congregation strove mightily to lure the Native population away from the Russian Orthodox church, where, oddly enough, only Russian and Latin were used, though most of their congregation spoke neither.

It was the contention of the Kenai Chapel faction that since nobody understood anything that was said during Mass at the Russian church, they were not learning the way of salvation there and must be proselytized. The town chose sides and dug in. As a general rule, whites with a religious bent attended the Kenai Chapel, while Natives attended the Russian church. A few of them became members of the Chapel and were real "stars in the crown" of the missionaries. However, if they got mad at the preacher, they'd go back to the Russian church, and so it was a constant tug-of-war.

My folks, of course, joined the Chapel. There I continued my religious training, attending Sunday School without fail (I have a lapel pin for four years' perfect attendance), worship services on Sunday mornings AND Sunday evenings, Bible study and prayer meeting on Wednesday nights, and later, Kenai Youth Fellowship (KYF) on Fridays. When we first moved to Kenai, the Chapel was presided over by two missionaries named Violet Able and Olga Erickson, who along with the usual services also held a weekly Christian storybook hour for younger kids. Our favorite books were those written by a man named Paul Hutchins, the Sugar Creek Gang adventure series.

It was Olga, with her guitar, who taught me to harmonize. I took to it immediately and enthusiastically, my favorite hymn being Page 111 in the old green hymnal: "At Calvary." But a few months after we arrived in town, Vi and Olga moved on to other fields of harvest, and Walt and Eldy Covich took their place.

Eldy was one hot piano player. She was a great improviser, and we knew she could easily be a professional Ragtime Joe, except, of course, that she didn't play ragtime, more's the pity. Walt played the trombone, and both of them sang well. Not as well as Mrs. Munson, a buxom lady with a set of lungs like a bellows who performed only at special functions: school programs, graduations, and the occasional wedding or funeral. But then Mrs. Munson had had voice lessons, and, it was rumored, even operatic training. She was awesome.

My piano lessons with Eldy went well. Hymns are generally easy to play, and since they were my only music besides the John Thompson series for beginners, I learned to play hymns. I never approached Eldy's level of skill, but I did get competent enough to take her place on the piano bench, humbly and on the rare occasions when she was absent, to accompany the congregation. I gradually worked my way up to simple old-fashioned ditties but never mastered anything remotely current or advanced. Dad mumbled frequently under his breath that I had absolutely no sense of timing and the heaviest loud-pedal foot he'd ever heard. He was right.

The Kenai Chapel became our primary social outlet, as well as our religious home. Although members were not allowed to smoke, drink, dance, play cards, attend movies or wear any but the faintest of cosmetics, we did have some grand times. Besides special music, we occasionally attempted plays and programs. We held Easter breakfasts, and fellowship evenings. Once in a while a visiting missionary would come to town, causing quite a stir. After the coffee and cake that followed the evening service, we'd all join hands in a circle and solemnly sing "God Be With You 'Til We Meet Again" to the visitor. This often brought tears to the eye.

As I grew older, I began to resent that as a member of the Kenai Chapel, and therefore An Example, I wasn't allowed to do many things the other kids were doing. Somebody had begun showing old movies a couple times a month in a deserted hall, but I didn't get to see them. Our school held occasional dances, but I couldn't go. Since I didn't have any desire to smoke, drink or play cards, those prohibitions didn't bother me, but I rebelled in my teens and started wearing lipstick and mascara. The subject of sex was never spoken of directly in Chapel discussions, but we knew it was a huge no-no, too.

I decided that if I ever got away from Kenai, I would simply try to keep the Big Ten commandments and the Lord's admonition to "love thy neighbor as thyself." As for the rest, I, like St. Paul, would practice "moderation in all things." But I wonder if those Chapel restrictions are perhaps one reason I eventually made the biggest mistake of my life. Of which you will learn more, later.

My folks became pillars of the Kenai Chapel. Mom taught Sunday school, Dad helped with maintenance, they tithed. By the time I was

12, I was teaching Sunday School, too, as well as daily vacation Bible school in the summer.

Our old Chapel was a small frame building overlooking Da Bank with a red sign warning "Prepare To Meet Thy God" painted at the roof line. More than one bush pilot admitted that that sign sure got his attention as he made his approach to the Kenai airfield. Built on a slight incline, the Chapel took a nose dive toward the pulpit, which was an inadvertent blessing since it enabled those sitting on folding chairs in the rear to better see what was going on up front.

We enjoyed our services. How we sang! In the years since, I've never been in a church where "Beulah Land" and "I'll Be a Sunbeam" were sung with more gusto. The Chapel, with all its prohibitions, was a force to be reckoned with in Kenai, and was, for better and worse, a large influence in my life.

My parents were totally non-confrontational, peace-loving people. I heard them argue loudly only once, and that upset me so badly I ran crying from my bedroom to beg them to stop. Which they immediately did. It was probably their pacifistic attitude that caused them to simply go along with the Chapel's dictates. And I suppose they thought it was best to err on the side of righteousness, if err one must. I know my mother agreed that the restrictions placed on Chapel members were too severe, but she bowed to the dictum that "you are either with us or you are against us," and opted to be "with us." Thus we tried our best to be, if not actually Examples, at least not Stumbling Blocks. It wasn't easy, especially for a young person. And it wasn't always possible.

Meanwhile, I was learning to adjust to Kenai ways. I found a best friend in Evelyn Baktuit, a girl with beautiful wiry red hair, freckles, and a fine patrician nose. Her uncle, George Miller Jr., was a leader of the Kenaitze tribe and later, after passage of the Alaska Native Claims Settlement Act, the first president of CIRI (Cook Inlet Region, Inc.). Evelyn and I were inseparable for about four years, until we got to high school, and then, regrettably, we drifted apart. Maybe we just had too much togetherness, but we also had great fun. I'm happy to say we did resume our friendship 30-some years and many miles later.

In our front yard, near Da Bank, there was in those days a huge spruce tree. Its branches made a natural sanctuary, which became our playhouse. Evelyn and I filled it with junk from you-know-where. We

Evelyn Baktuit

had a couch, a chair, and a table, and "running water" was provided from a five-gallon gas can with attached spigot. To add to the fun and intrigue of our playhouse, just beyond the wire fence were the three old graves I glimpsed from my bedroom, surrounded by a weathered, rotting wood fence.

The story was that these graves dated back to the time of the Russian occupation of Kenai, then known as Fort St. Nicholas, in 1791. One of the graves contained, so it was said, the remains of a man who had developed gangrene in his big toe. He finally got up the courage to have the toe amputated, but the infection had already spread up his leg. The leg had to be severed at the knee, and as the gangrene progressed, eventually at the groin. A wooden leg was somehow attached to take the place of the severed leg, but it was too late. The man died. They buried him, wooden leg in place, and in due time, a tree sprouted from the wooden leg and grew above his grave.

This was not the tree under which we built our playhouse, but it was right next door, and it was obvious to us that it was a very special tree. We discussed the possibility of digging up the graves to see what was left, but Mom warned us that this was against the law, so we contented ourselves with digging up a mound in the front yard where there had reportedly once stood a Russian cannon emplacement. I believe the story is true because that would have been an excellent vantage point, overlooking both the mouth of the Kenai River and Cook Inlet. We found several pieces of iron cannon balls before we tired of that strenuous activity and went back to playing in our playhouse under the tree, beside Pegleg's grave.

We frequently and very carefully made our way down Da Bank to the beach below. During the summer it was fun to collect seashells (very small, un-exotic-looking ones), or to sketch with a stick of driftwood on the sand life-sized plans of the grand homes we would one day own. Sometimes, in a fit of missionary zeal, we printed huge messages on the beach with our driftwood: "Jesus Saves," or "Where Will You Spend Eternity??" At other times, we informed the whole town that "Jack Loves Carol," or "Sally Kissed Robert." Our news flashes remained spread across the beach in letters 15 feet tall until the next high tide.

Sometimes we helped ourselves to a handful of the religious tracts left on a table in the entrance hall of the Chapel and then, using discarded bottles from Da Bank below one of the bars in town, we'd stuff the tracts into the bottles, tightly cork the necks, and toss them into the inlet, where, we fervently prayed, some heathen or wicked seafaring man would recover one of them and find the Lord.

Once a year the hooligan migrated up the river. "Hooligan" is the Alaska name for the smelt *Thaleichthys pacificus,* which Chinook Jargon called *oolachon* (now spelled *eulachon*) and which we pronounced delicious. Young people rushed to the beach with nets, scooping up hooligan by the dozens. Some we took home to our families, but many were skewered onto green sticks, to be cooked over a bonfire and devoured right there at the water's edge. If somebody remembered to bring along a few potatoes to throw into the fire and roast, so much the better.

After the river froze solid each winter, we often saw moose picking their way over the snow-covered ice. We kids weren't often tempted to go to the beach when it was so cold and miserable. However, when spring breakup approached, the snow melted off the ice and presently the ice itself began breaking up and floating out into the inlet. With many a loud groan and crash, with *cracks* loud as gunshots, the ice broke into gigantic floes and passed beneath our village, a majestic, frozen flotilla. Day and night for weeks the pandemonium continued, but it was music to our ears, for we knew that winter was over and spring would not be far behind.

With the advent of breakup, Kenai also began to stir again. Realizing that spring and summer passed all too quickly, and that there was much to be accomplished during the long days, everyone shook off winter lethargy, shed long johns, and set about springtime chores.

Evelyn and I, tired of sledding and skating at Beaver Dam, always longed to head for the beach again. One fine breakup day we pulled on our knee-high rubber boots and descended, slipping and sliding through melting patches of snow and emerging plots of muck and mire, down Da Bank.

We set up housekeeping on one of the ice floes—a tremendous houseboat, if you will. It had moored itself tight to the beach, so we felt safely grounded. As we became more lost in our fantasy world, however, we suddenly realized that our mansion had pulled free of its berth and was slowly joining the armada of icebergs headed toward

Cook Inlet. Evelyn bravely jumped off, but I hesitated, afraid the water was higher than my boots. Yelling and splashing along the beach, Evelyn ordered me to jump. Her fervor convinced me that it was better to get ice water in my boots than to perish in the Pacific. I jumped, and sure enough, my boots filled with the coldest water this side of the Pole. I got a scolding that evening for having wet boots, but I didn't tell Mom how they got that way.

During the long, dark Alaskan winters, we spent a lot of time listening to the radio. Thrillers like "The Shadow" and "The Green Hornet" were my favorites. And every Sunday after morning church services, we hurried home to listen to "Hawaii Calls," brought to us from the Royal Hawaiian Hotel on beautiful Waikiki Beach. I didn't dream I'd ever answer Hawaii's call, but I've made almost a dozen visits so far. Dad sometimes listened to opera late on Saturday evenings, a practice that both surprised and dismayed me, for I definitely preferred country-western music. Still do, for that matter.

There was one program that everyone in town listened to every night. It originated from studios in Anchorage and was called "Mukluk Telegraph." In those days, without telephones and with very slow mail delivery, Alaskans were isolated in their far-flung villages. Someone who wanted to send a message to a friend in another village would contact the people at Mukluk Telegraph, and that evening the message would go forth to the entire territory:

"Joe in Nome wants Harry in Nenana to know that his dory was found beached but seaworthy."

"Anastasia Barikoff sends love to Alex in Sitka, with the news that he's the father of an 8-pound, 3-ounce baby boy."

"Jake Miller in Homer wants Henrietta to know that all is forgiven and she should come home before the road snows in."

And a few days later: "Henrietta sends word to Jake in Homer that she and Dudley already have tickets on the next Alaska Steamship out of Seward."

It was better stuff than you find on soap operas these days. And it was for real. We never missed it.

Another radio favorite was a country-western program featuring a disc jockey who played requests. True, the records were usually some years behind the Top 40 hits in the States, but we loved 'em. If you had a special request for your sweetie, you just dropped a letter to the

Still "the best view in the world"—looking from Erik Hansen Memorial Park across Cook Inlet toward volcanoes Iliamna and Redoubt, winter 2002, and upriver from Kenai, summer 1993

station in Anchorage, and eventually you'd hear your tune, along with your message, e.g., "Boris sends Judy a big kiss and wants her to know, 'I'm Movin' On'." Well now, that's interesting!

Evelyn and I somehow became aware that the young wife of one of the Kenai fishermen was playing hanky-panky with a construction worker while her husband was away tending his fish site. To our earnest little minds, this was not a thing to be tolerated. After giving it some (not enough) thought, we mailed a request: "Slippin' Around," to "Magdaline from her secret admirer." It didn't occur to us that if said husband, who was known to have a hair-trigger temper, heard that request, he might very well catch the next tide home and blow both Maggie and her secret admirer to Kingdom Come. It didn't occur to us until after the request was in the mail, and then we began to worry.

We spent several miserable days praying the letter wouldn't arrive, that our request would not be read on the air, or that the fisherman would be out picking his nets while "Slippin' Around" was telling the world that his Magdaline had a secret admirer.

As the days crawled by, we became more frightened. Finally one evening we heard the request on the air. Even now I feel my heart beat fast to remember it. There followed a week of the most painful anticipation for us two tattle-tales. We carefully watched the house where we imagined the unfaithful wife cowering in fear. We listened for gunshots. We scanned the beach for the husband's dory.

But thank the Lord, nothing happened. Maybe we got the miracle we prayed for. Maybe everybody in Kenai was struck deaf during the playing of our request. I don't know, but that couple was still married the last I heard. I don't know what happened to the secret admirer, either.

Sometimes Evelyn and I engaged in less dangerous pursuits. Mom had several barrels of old clothes that she kept in the attic of our cabin. We spent hours up there, dressing like movie stars and painting our faces with forbidden makeup. One day we stuffed "our" bras with Kleenex, donned some glad-rags, painted our lips and cheeks, and then, in a fit of brazen audacity, dared each other to walk over to Casey Jones' grocery store to buy a candy bar. Giggling and jiggling, we made our purchase, with arms crossed over our padded bosoms. Casey, to his credit, pretended he didn't recognize us, and treated us as if we were new ladies in town.

Halloween was another opportunity to dress up. We gave a great deal of thought and effort to our costumes, which of course had to be homemade. We had some huge successes, and some disasters. The successes I've forgotten, but the disasters remain forever burned in my brain.

One year we concocted our costumes from crepe paper. All went well the first part of the evening as we raced around town trick-or-treating, but then it started to rain, though not nearly enough to cause us to give up our begging. Days were growing short by October 31st and it was dark as we scurried through the drizzle. We didn't notice until people started laughing when they opened their doors that our costumes had become sodden and in the process had run. Our skin and underclothes were dyed bright shades of blue, red, yellow and green. Human Easter eggs.

Another year we were delighted to receive popcorn balls from one of our benefactors. Neither of us had ever had one. As we ran toward the next house, I tripped over my costume and fell. My treasured pop-corn ball flipped out of my bag and landed square in the middle of a mud puddle. A total loss. Evelyn generously shared hers with me—it was fan-tastic!

Still another Halloween, we were running full tilt through the dark from house to house when we simultaneously crashed into a bar-ricade nailed to two upright posts. We fell to the ground as if struck by lightning, the wind knocked right out of us. For several minutes we writhed there, gasping helplessly for breath, sure we were going to die, and afraid we weren't.

Nevertheless, Halloween remained one of our favorite holidays.

On summer evenings, when the sun shone bright till long past winter bedtime, Kenai kids gathered for play. Some kid-type radar told us where the action was; we always managed to find the group no matter which end of town they were converging on. Anti-anti-over (remembered variously as Aunty-aunty-over and even Annie-Annie-over) was fun if we could find a house where the owner didn't mind our throwing a rubber ball over the roof. Hide-and-seek was too old-fashioned. We preferred Kick-the-Can. Since we were just beginning to notice the differences between boys and girls, the idea was to hide with a favored member of the opposite sex and maybe sneak a little kiss before you were required to race forward and kick the can.

During that period of our development, passing notes became an obsession. "Couples" had secret hiding places (holes in tree trunks, a metal Band-aid box under the Chapel steps, a loose shingle on the back wall of the school house), where they left messages for their beloved. Very often a younger brother or sister would sneak after a youthful Lothario, discover the hidey-hole and broadcast the contents of the notes to the whole world. We tried to keep our identities secret by never using our names, just our initials. As if everybody in town didn't know that A.R. was Arlene Rheingans and G.H. was Georgie Hunter.

Often we couldn't wait to slip a note in the secret place and instead folded it into a tiny wad and tossed it to our heart-throb during class. The trick was to accomplish this without having the note intercepted by (a) a friend, (b) an enemy, or worst of all, (c) the teacher, who would dramatically unfold it and read it to the entire class. This happened a few times to A.R., and I'm here to tell you, it was mortifying. Not enough to make us stop passing notes, though. I'm a bit embarrassed (and mystified) to find several of these ancient memos in my possession as I write.

The boys weren't always in a romantic mood. Sometimes they were downright mean, especially after the first snowfall, when they couldn't control the primal urge to hurl snowballs at the heads of erstwhile girlfriends.

The first time I wore my new navy-blue pants suit to school, I took the shortcut through the woods. Suddenly I was attacked by a gang of snowball-throwing boys. I took off running like a hare, dodging past the Nesses' house and through their back yard, where I tripped over a piece of wood and went crashing on my face. There wasn't a lot of snow on the ground, only an inch or so—enough to just barely cover an abandoned toilet hole that had filled to capacity and was almost level with the ground. A new hole had been dug conveniently nearby and the privy was simply moved over it. Someone had failed to cover the old hole with dirt, and I fell flat into it. I never cared much for the blue pants suit after that.

Even scarier than snowball throwers were the knife toters. Many of the Kenai kids carried some form of knife at all times. They never actually stabbed anybody that I know of, but several times knives were drawn during fights or heated arguments, and one big boy pulled a knife on the principal once.

The boys also carried kitchen matches. Sitting behind a girl in class, they'd sometimes poke her fanny with a pencil, and when she reached back to shoo them off they'd burn her fingers with a match. I still carry a scar on my right thumb.

One day a particularly obnoxious teen-age boy got mad at Evelyn and me. Who knows why? We were only about 10 or 11, while he was old enough to shave. At any rate, he chased us through the snow to the girls' outhouse behind the school. We barely had time to slam and lock the door before he began pounding and kicking it. "I'm gonna cut you up," he yelled as he stalked back and forth in the snow, getting colder and madder by the minute.

We were pretty cold, too, but had sense enough to sit tight in our stinky refuge until, peeking through the cracks, we saw him stomp away. Then we ran to my house, sniveling and choking on our fear and indignation. Mom walked us back to school and had a talk with the principal, and that was the end of that.

One of the most dangerous things about living in Kenai, besides Da Bank caving in, floating icebergs, moose and bear attacks, and boys with snowballs and knives, was the fact that for many years we had no medical facilities. We did have one or two former nurses living on homesteads who did what they could in a pinch. If someone was seriously injured, though, a call would go forth to Anchorage by shortwave radio, and the 10th Rescue Squadron would fly in to pick up the patient.

Anyone who couldn't sit up in the helicopter was placed in a wire mesh coffin-like contraption and strapped to the outside of the chopper. I swore I'd rather die in my own bed, or in a ditch for that matter, than fly strapped to the exterior of a helicopter all the way to Anchorage. Fortunately, I never had to prove it, for although I had several bad boo-boos, Mom or somebody usually patched me up.

Once, my left index finger became infected while I was cleaning salmon in the creek. Several days later, red and blue lines appeared running up my arm, and the finger swelled mightily. Mom sent for Mandy Walker to come take a look. Mandy was Pappy Walker's second wife; Jessebelle had divorced him and moved back to the States.

Arlene and Ruth Grueninger cleaning fish at Kenai

Maybe she was scared of bears, or maybe she just got tired of Pappy calling everybody "Hon." Anyway, Mandy was a sweet, gray-haired former nurse.

She arrived at our cabin, took a look (and a sniff) at my putrid finger and set right to work. First she soaked it in the hottest water I could stand, then she soaked it again in some kind of disinfectant. Then she packed ointment all around the finger, covered it with gauze, then wrapped the entire arm in hot wet towels. She topped the whole thing off with a piece of an old oilcloth table cover. She poked a needle of penicillin in my rump and then sat down beside my bed to see if I'd make it. I can still smell her perfume as she hovered above me. Evening in Paris.

This "fish poisoning" was a common occurrence in Kenai, and if not treated promptly and properly could get nasty. Left untreated long enough, you could end up like Pegleg with a tree growing out of your grave.

When I was in seventh or eighth grade, after the new school had been built, I required Mandy's services again. When construction was finished on the school, many odds and ends of materials were left lying about. We didn't have a gym or playground equipment, so naturally the kids played with whatever they could find. This was a time when everyone was flying-saucer crazy. The whole country was hooked on little green men from Mars.

The wooden tops of nail kegs make dandy flying saucers, we learned, and our boys could throw them with great power but little accuracy, as I found out one day at recess when I crouched down to talk to a younger child. Kapow! The next thing I knew I was face down on the playground. As I sat up and touched the back of my throbbing head, blood ran down my arm and dripped off my elbow. Instead of going into the school for help I followed my instincts, and like a wounded animal started dragging myself toward home. I hadn't gotten far when Marshal Petersen came along in his gray Buick, pressed his handkerchief to my wound and drove me to my mother.

Mom did what she could but also sent for Mandy, who shaved a nice bald patch around the gaping wound on my scalp. They debated about stitches, but I didn't like the sound of that and persuaded Mandy to "butterfly" it with medical tape. Luckily for me, the tape held. I still have a lumpy scar beneath my hair—and possibly the distinction of being the first Earthling attacked by a flying saucer.

Later, in high school, I slipped into an icy rut in the road and broke my ankle. It hurt like the dickens, but I thought it was just a "dislocation" and limped home, where I tried stomping on it good and hard to snap it back into place. This was not one of my brighter ideas. In a few days the ankle swelled to a remarkable size and turned an ominous shade of midnight blue. I was hauled to the hospital in Seward—over wash-boardy, gravel roads, leg throbbing every mile of the way—for X-rays and a toes-to-knee cast that not only helped my ankle mend but enabled me to kick-start my motor scooter more easily.

The cast did, however, hamper my progress as I tearfully climbed down Da Bank to retrieve the body of my beloved Tuffy. Along with a number of other dogs, he had been shot and dumped like garbage by some local bullies. I buried him in our yard, not far from the three ancient graves.

Other animals in my little pet cemetery eventually included wild birds, an occasional chicken or rabbit that had died of undetermined causes and was therefore un-eatable, and a series of silver-dollar-sized turtles, all named George. Every so often various friends and I would dig up these deceased critters to see how their mortal remains were faring. I planned to go into medicine in those days, and felt it my bounden duty to expose myself to as much blood and gore as possible. Once, having dug up a late chicken, I pulled a worm from the carcass and chased a good friend, Mildred Kooly, around and around our house. Poor Millie tripped and broke her leg. Or arm. She reminded me of this episode nearly 50 years later, and since I don't remember it at all, I think I intentionally blocked the details from my mind out of sheer mortification.

During those years when there were no medical facilities nearby, we were twice visited by a U.S. government medical ship, the *M.V. Hygiene,* which moored down by Dobinspeck's cannery. During its weeklong stay, everyone in town was invited to go aboard for checkups, shots, X-rays, and whatever else was available. The second time the health ship came, I was in my early teens and fascinated with all things medical. I was allowed to work aboard the *Hygiene* as an appointment clerk, and I thought I'd died and gone to Heaven.

I had all the tests and shots they'd allow, including a test that made us question the competence of the entire program. I had suffered off and on with vaginitis since I was three, and after the doctor on the *Hygiene* examined me, he prescribed yet another medication. Several days later the ship sailed on to other ports. In a few weeks my parents received word from the health officials in Juneau that I, and an even younger girl, had syphilis. The other girl's parents and mine immediately took us to Seward, where we were examined and tested again. The results disproved the *Hygiene* doctor's diagnosis. Our mothers demanded and got a retraction and an apology from the ship's doctor, and our medical records were duly corrected.

Our family customarily made a trip to Seward once a year or so for physical and dental checkups. I dreaded those visits—not because I didn't like the doctors, dentists and nurses (they were my heroes)—but because of the trip itself. The roads were rough and dusty and I became miserably carsick as soon as we drove out of town. Mom insisted that singing helped divert one's attention from the nausea, so between bouts of biliousness, we sang until we were hoarse. I always marveled when I got a good report at my check-ups, feeling as lousy as I did.

Fortunately, I had teeth that didn't require more than a small filling now and then. When I was around 12, though, I got a terrific toothache, a real wall-banger. For some reason Dad decided not to take me to Seward, but instead sought out the services of old Doc Pollard, a retired dentist who homesteaded in Kasilof, some 15 or 20 miles south of Kenai.

Dad and I, in the seldom-used pickup, arrived at Doc's place, off the main road, and were told by Doc's wife that he was out in the barn tending the cow. She ushered us into their house, where we sat, silent and apprehensive, on a dusty old horsehair couch. Prominently displayed in the front room was a venerable "dentist chair" that looked suspiciously like a barber chair. As the minutes crept by, Dad became fidgety. Finally he said he'd go out and talk to Doc, and told me, "You wait here, Kid."

It seemed like hours before Doc, in his coveralls and rubber boots, came clumping in. Alone. He may have washed his hands, but I didn't see him do it. He motioned me to climb onto the chair and told me to open my mouth. After considerable poking and prodding, hmmmmming and head-shaking, he took a raggedy black bag from beneath the velveteen-covered end table and dug out a few tools of the trade.

Before he could fill the tooth, he had to drill it. Doc seemed to enjoy his drill work. His drill was operated by foot-pedal power. He pumped and pedaled and drilled while smoke and tooth dust poured out of my mouth and Dad sat out in the pickup with the windows rolled up. I tried to believe Dad simply couldn't bear to see or hear me hurt. I still try to believe that.

My experience with Doc Pollard turned out to be a blessing. Not only did the filling cure my toothache, but for the rest of my life I have never been afraid to go to a dentist. I figure nothing could be worse than that encounter. As extra insurance, I tell the story to every new dentist I visit, and I like to think they are so overcome with sympathy that they try extra hard to be gentle.

It just occurred to me why I might have had that terrible cavity. For several years I'd been saving Sugar Daddy coupons to receive a "mystery prize." Sugar Daddys were, and maybe are for all I know, a sweet caramel confection on a stick. With the consistency of plastic, they stuck to your teeth like Superglue. If you succeeded in biting directly into one, it could pull your teeth right out of your gums. Within their yellow and red wrappers were cards or coupons. When you saved 50 of those, you were guaranteed a super-colossal mystery prize. With every spare nickel I could get my hands on I rushed to Casey's store, or up to the Kenai Commercial, and purchased a Sugar Daddy.

Partway into the process, after consuming about 35 Sugar Daddys, I grew to loathe the beastly things. I persevered, though, and the day finally arrived when I had accumulated the requisite 50 coupons. I filled out the order form, carefully counted my coupons several times, and mailed them to the candy company headquarters, somewhere Outside.

Then the long wait began. It took forever to have things shipped to Alaska in those days, because everything came by boat. Slow boat via China. Months passed, and finally one day there arrived in the mail a long box for me. I tore it open with trembling hands and beheld my stupendous surprise: a giant, one-pound Sugar Daddy.

I was forever sending away for something. It took me a long time to learn. Secret decoder rings and genuine Foreign Legion compasses never half lived up to my expectations. The ads on the inside covers of comic books always looked so inviting. Once I sent for a gizmo that, using double mirrors, promised to allow me to copy any picture accurately, to the last detail. Ha! But who needs gizmos to create beauty? I replied to the ad that said, "DRAW ME," hoping I'd be invited to attend the famous art institute advertised, but apparently my rendering of the pretty girl's profile wasn't good enough. No invitation was forthcoming. Nevertheless, I continued to send away and to hope. The anticipation of receiving something wonderful in the mail was enough to keep me going.

When I left Mrs. Petersen's third-grade class and advanced to the room across the hall at the old school, I was taught by her daughter, Peggy Arness. Again there were several grades in a single room. It soon became apparent that I was bored stiff with the fourth grade curriculum, so Peggy and Mom arranged for me to skip directly into the fifth. Since I was now the youngest child in the class, I had to stretch to keep up. We had a couple of boys in the room who shaved already. I was now in the same grade as my buddy, Evelyn, which made me very happy, but school was never again as easy for me. Geography and Roman numerals were both fourth-grade subjects; I've never been up to snuff on them.

Classes were small, though, so we received a lot of individual attention from our teachers. We didn't have the sophisticated teaching aids and lab materials available in stateside schools, but I feel I made up for that lack by reading everything I could get my hands on. I cannot over-stress the importance and joy of reading. When Kenai finally acquired a modest library I was one of its best customers, and I believe the adage that the person who doesn't read is no better off than the person who can't read.

Further, I was blessed with a mother who enjoyed helping me with my schoolwork. She helped me memorize "The Midnight Ride of Paul Revere," and didn't mind staying up until midnight, drilling the classifications of the animal kingdom into my brain: Monotremata, Marsupials, Insectivora, Carnivora . . . She once remarked that she learned as much when I was in school as she did when *she* went to school.

Mom was a good, patient teacher. We enjoyed each other's company and, without forgetting who was mother and who was child, who made the rules and who followed them, we were also good friends. Since our social life was so limited, we tried to find new ways of entertaining ourselves and each other.

When the women of the area started a Homemakers' Club, Mom was a charter member. I felt so bad at being left out that Mom asked if I could come to the meetings occasionally. Nobody objected (maybe they were pleased to have another warm body in the room), so soon I was almost a regular. The ladies discussed such things as recipes, child rearing, sewing, fancywork, household budgets, and the challenges of making a home under somewhat primitive conditions. I learned an awful lot at those meetings and am grateful for the education.

Once or twice a year the Homemakers put on a program, and if called upon I'd perform in any way I was needed: extra singer in the chorus, sound effects, costume changer, even the child's role in a couple of their plays.

One play I particularly remember was more visual than vocal. Several of the women and I dressed up as hillbillies. The more outrageous the costumes, the better everyone liked them. The gist of the drama was that we were waiting at a railroad track. Every so often someone would come along and we'd ask, "What time is the next train to Chicago?" We'd be told, "7:38", and we'd pass the word along from one of us to the next and the next, shake our heads dramatically and wait until someone else came along. Same question, same answer passed down the line. Finally one passerby said casually, "Oh, so you're going to Chicago, are you?" Whereupon we all replied, "Oh, no, we're just waiting to cross the railroad tracks!" Tennessee Williams, look out. It brought down the house.

One evening when Dad was doing some maintenance at the fish site and Mom was attending Homemakers' Club alone, I went to bed early and had just fallen asleep when there was a racket at our door. I jumped up and opened the door to find several members of the club practically carrying Mom. They said the big coffee urn had up-ended and dumped a couple gallons of scalding hot coffee in her lap. Then they all went back to the meeting. I helped Mom out of her clothes and surveyed the damage. We didn't have anything suitable for a burn of that nature and size, and no way to contact Mandy, but I remembered reading in *Sue Barton, Student Nurse* a remedy Sue had used when she was in a similar fix. I made a pot of strong tea, cooled it quickly in the snow, dipped dishtowels into the cold tea and applied them to Mom's abdomen.

That Sue Barton knew what she was doing; in no time Mom felt much better, and the burns healed nicely.

Mom and I liked to go for walks in the long summer evenings. Sometimes we'd walk along the marshland down by the beach. As we walked we'd glance back at our shoeprints and notice how quickly they filled with a rainbow-hued liquid. We thought it was real pretty, not realizing that one of the very first oil discoveries in Alaska would be made right there near Kenai several years later. I'm glad all that oil business happened after I left, because it completely changed my hometown, and not for the better, I'm afraid.

We also liked to walk through the cemeteries. In keeping with the prevailing attitude, there were two cemeteries in town. One, over by the airstrip, was referred to as the American Cemetery, while the other was close to the Russian Orthodox church and was, naturally, known as the Russian Cemetery. Again, those of mixed backgrounds were free to choose where they wanted to be planted when their time came.

We thought the Russian Cemetery was much more interesting. It was at the north edge of town, reached by a short dirt road and fairly well hidden by trees, bushes and weeds. Many of the graves were covered with little rectangular houses, and topped with the distinctive Russian cross. Some were painted bright colors, but the older ones were weathered gray and falling to ruin. It was the custom at Easter and Christmas for relatives of the departed to leave food and small gifts at these little houses. Of course, we Kenai Chapel people didn't subscribe to that idea at all, but I secretly found it quite charming.

One evening it was beginning to get dark as Mom and I wandered through the Russian Cemetery. Tuffy was off doing dog things somewhere nearby when suddenly the stillness of the night was broken by the most blood-curdling howls. Mom and I nearly knocked each other down trying to get out of there when it dawned on us that maybe we weren't being haunted after all. In fact, the racket sounded more canine than ghostly. When Tuffy didn't come at my call, we went looking for him. He wasn't too hard to locate, making that uproar, and we soon discovered why he was so indignant. He'd gotten caught in a rabbit snare that held him fast by the hind leg. Once released, he was as good as new.

Harriet Mann and Tuffy

Mom and I laughed all the way home, and I believe those cemetery visits were the beginning of my lifelong appreciation of graveyards. I think they're among the most peaceful, comforting, dignified, to say nothing of just plain interesting, places on Earth, and always welcome an opportunity to stroll through one.

Death was a frequent visitor to Kenai. As I've mentioned, TB was a familiar killer, but besides natural deaths were many accidental ones. A number of the kids I went to school with died young from drownings, hunting mishaps, car wrecks, fires and other accidents. People often lived or worked in isolated areas, far from town, and even in town, as I said, there was very little immediate medical help available.

We had no funeral parlor, no undertaker, no caskets, no florists to ease the burden on those remaining. When someone died, a simple wooden coffin was made, the body was washed and wrapped in a sheet, services were held at the Chapel or the Russian church, and mourners walked, carrying the coffin to the appropriate cemetery where friends had dug the grave and the deceased was laid to rest.

Being the kind of kid I was, nosy, imaginative and curious, I never missed a funeral. And then I'd get so spooked I couldn't sleep at night, and I'd promise myself I'd never go to another. But as soon as the occasion arose, I was the first mourner at the bier.

Shortly after we moved to Kenai, a local woman passed away. Her family chose to have her services in the Chapel. I went early to assure I'd get a good seat. When I arrived, Olga, the missionary at that time, was the only other person there. The coffin was closed, so I moseyed on up front and leaned against it while making small talk with Olga. Suddenly Olga said with a twinkle, "Do you want to pay your last respects?" and before I could say, "Hold on there!" she opened the lid of the box. That time I didn't sleep for a week.

The next incident involved a young local fellow, still in his teens. He was a strange guy, always teasing the other kids in a mean kind of way. I didn't care much for him, and in fact was more than a little afraid of him. His family had a fish site, and he fished commercially with them every summer. One year when I was around nine or 10, he fell overboard while picking nets. He was struck in the head by the propeller and killed; his body wasn't found for several days.

It happens that at that time my folks had gone into partnership with the missionaries on a food freezer. We didn't have electricity yet, but the missionaries had a private power plant, so the freezer was kept in their garage. Mom asked me to run over and get a pound of moose-burger for dinner. I skipped to the Chapel compound and let myself into the dim, cold garage. Feeling my way over to the freezer, I stubbed my toe on something large and squishy lying on the floor. They had finally found the body, wrapped it in a blanket, and were storing it in the missionary's garage until a coffin could be built. I tore home without the moosemeat and we had canned salmon for dinner that night.

Mrs. Mathers, an elderly lady who homesteaded a few miles from Kenai, was one of our more colorful characters. She and her husband, with some chickens and a couple of goats, had arrived from the States in a covered wagon shortly after the Alcan Highway was opened to civilian traffic, somewhere around 1945. Not long after their arrival at Kenai, the Mister died, leaving Mrs. Mathers to homestead all on her own. Apparently she built, or finished building, a rough cabin, and proceeded to clear the required land.

Several times a year Mrs. M. would walk into town to do her errands, including a stop at the post office to collect her mail and visit with my mom. She told Mom that she saw strange lights at night, and that she was sure she was being watched. When Mom asked who might be watching her, Mrs. Mathers replied without hesitation that it was "the Communists." "But why would the Communists be watching you?" Mom wondered. "They want to find out how old I am, of course," was her answer. Apparently another Aunt Ivy.

One day Mrs. Mathers took the notion that she wanted to work at Libby's cannery during salmon canning season. She rode across the river in the dory with Libby's mail carrier, had an interview with the personnel manager, and was turned down because of her advanced age. This made her hopping mad, and she seethed all the way back to our side of the river. (This we learned later.)

That afternoon Evelyn and I were playing in the back yard when Mom leaned out the post office window and yelled for us to go see what was happening down Da Bank a ways. People were beginning to congregate, peering over the bluff toward the beach. We raced over to check out the action, and there on the beach below us lay Mrs. Mathers, stretched out stone dead. Marshal Petersen's jeep was already there; he was interrogating Libby's mail carrier, while his deputy took notes. Apparently her temper tantrum had triggered a fatal heart attack.

Presently the men took a gray blanket with a wide black stripe from the jeep, wrapped Mrs. Mather's body in it, deposited her in the jeep, and off they drove.

Hearing that Mrs. M. was to be buried from the Kenai Chapel was great news to me, for I intended to be there on two counts: First, I knew she didn't have any relatives or friends around and needed all the mourners she could get, and secondly, I wanted to find out how old she was. I figured if it was important to the Communists, it behooved me to get the facts.

When the appointed day and hour rolled around, I was down on the beach, gathering shells and rocks for my collection. Glancing at my watch, I saw I had just enough time to climb Da Bank and present myself at the Chapel.

I was surprised and gratified to see a few other attendees, and since I was just a tad late, I wiggled onto one of the folding chairs at the very back of the room. I also wasn't taking any chances on having the coffin lid popped open again. The missionary gave a real nice eulogy. So nice, and so touching, I felt my eyes begin to fill, and my nose started running. I reached into the pocket of my blue jeans, pulled out my handkerchief, and to my horror, all my new rocks and shells tumbled out with a clatter and rolled down the slanted floor to the front of the room, under the coffin.

Everybody in the place, which included my mother, jumped in fright and turned around and glared at me. I was so mortified I forgot to listen when Mrs. M's age was announced. Mom said later she was also too preoccupied at that moment to notice.

It seems to me that for a period of about four years, between my eighth and twelfth year, I had an unfortunate amount of contact with dead people. Several instances left a lasting effect on me.

One Sunday as Mom gave me my breakfast before Sunday School, she motioned to a car sitting in our horseshoe-shaped driveway. The motor was running, and she said the car had been there when she got up earlier to stoke the fire. She thought at first it was someone getting his mail in the post office attached to our cabin. As I ate my cereal, I peered out the window in front of the table, trying to recall whose car it was. There weren't very many vehicles in town, and most of them were familiar to us since they were driven to the post office regularly.

Oh well, we figured, maybe it was someone parking in our driveway while he ran across the road to Herman Hermansen's place. Deep snow covered most of the village, and only the main roads were cleared for traffic. Our road and driveway were always cleared because "the mail must go through."

As she helped me on with my boots and parka, Mom suggested, "Just take a peek inside and see if you can tell who that car belongs to." And off I went. As I approached the car, I could tell it had been there quite a while, for the air reeked with the smell of exhaust and the hard-packed snow directly under the car was completely melted. I marched up to the driver's door and grabbed hold of the handle so I could put my nose against the window and peer in. Two people slumped in the front seat, a man and a woman, both quite blue and obviously dead.

Mom, who was watching from the window, says I jumped straight into the air and hit the ground running. I nearly knocked our door down as I crashed into the cabin, racing for my folks' bedroom, yelling incoherently. Dad, who was sleeping soundly in his long underwear, with a knitted stocking cap on his head, moved faster than I ever saw him move, before or since. He hopped into his pants and boots and tore out to the car, with Mom and me right behind.

Opening the door, he reached in and turned off the motor. Then he gently touched the man, whose head was resting on the steering wheel, and the man slumped over against the woman's body. Dad said, "They're gone. Kid, go get the marshal."

There were only two women in town who had green coats like the one the woman in the car was wearing. One was the mother of some friends of mine, and the other was the 18-year-old sister of a little girl in my Sunday School class. Because the woman was slumped forward, with her face against the dashboard, I couldn't tell which one it was. I worried about it as I sped toward the Petersens' house. How the marshal understood my blathering I don't know, but he got the general idea and ordered me into his Buick.

When we arrived, a small crowd had gathered. Mom apparently didn't want me to see any more, and told me to go on to Sunday

School. I remember getting to my class just as it was letting out, seeing the little sister, and asking if Hazel had come home last night. "I don't think so," she said. "She wasn't in bed this morning." I was pretty sure I knew why, but I didn't say another word. I felt very sad.

It was established later that Hazel and a recently arrived young construction worker had been on a date. As many of the town sweethearts did, they parked in our driveway to talk, and because it was cold they left the motor running and the windows up. On the back seat a new muffler for the car was found, still in the box. He hadn't gotten around to putting it on.

When I got back from Sunday School, the bodies had been removed and the car was being towed away. A huge, dark scar in the shape of an automobile remained in the snow, until finally spring came and erased it. How I hated to come home alone from an evening function to see that black rectangle gleaming in the road ahead of me. I'd start singing "God Will Take Care of You" at the top of my lungs, and force myself to walk normally as long as possible. Then, when I could stand it no longer, I'd race around the spot and into the safety of our cabin.

Finding the bodies and living with that melted shadow all winter wasn't the end of the incident for me. Two days after the deaths, it was announced in school that the following afternoon, students attending Hazel's funeral at the Russian church would be excused from classes. This presented a moral dilemma for me. I wanted to go to that funeral. I felt I probably had as much right there as anybody, considering my role in the tragedy. And to be honest, I wanted to ditch school for the afternoon. The problem lay in the fact that as a loyal member of the Kenai Chapel, I understood clearly that I must never set foot in the Russian church. I was torn.

The next afternoon as the local kids solemnly donned their jackets and left the school, I joined them. We walked across town on the crystal-white new snow, and entered the hallowed, forbidden premises. The sanctuary was beautiful. Ancient icons and holy pictures gazed down at us from the walls. Incense hung heavy in the air. Dusty drapes and brocaded curtains separated us from the rear of the building, where I imagined all sorts of foreign and mysterious rites were performed by old Father Paul Shadura in his black robe, tall black priest's hat, and long, gray beard.

The funeral was taking place in the sanctuary. As soon as we entered, my classmates separated: Boys went to join the men standing to the right of the aisle, and girls joined the women to the left. There were no chairs or pews. I couldn't see much because the church was packed with winter-clad people, bulky in their woolens and parkas, but I could see in the center of the aisle, up front, the open coffin and Hazel, looking beautiful, lying therein.

Father Shadura, swinging the incense burner and chanting, moved slowly around the coffin as we took our places toward the rear. He was speaking in Russian or Latin, I guess. I couldn't tell the difference. I only knew that I felt very much out of my element, and regretted with all my heart that I'd come. The incense began to make my head spin; I was afraid I'd be sick. I stood my ground while Father rolled, scroll-like, a message to God and placed it in Hazel's pale hand. But when the mourners began filing past the wooden coffin, many bending to kiss the still face, I turned and made a break for the door.

I ran smack into the stomach of a woman standing right behind me, and was both terrified and comforted when she put her arms around me and held me tightly. I was further shocked when I looked up and saw my mother, and beside her our missionary's wife. They were the last two people I would have expected to encounter in the Russian Orthodox church, but Christian charity and compassion had compelled them to be there, to share the sorrow of Hazel's family and to ignore for once the rules of apartheid. I've often been happy to see my mother, but never more so than on that occasion.

Another death that moved me deeply occurred a few years after Hazel's. I'd come home from school and was sitting in our front room, embroidering a pillowcase. Again it was winter, so it was quite dark outside. Suddenly, my mother screamed from the post office: "Fire, fire! The Wickershams' trailer is on fire!"

The Wickershams were an old couple who lived in a small metal trailer house on the other side of our high chicken-wire fence, on the post office side of our place. Mrs. Wickersham was lame and hardly ever left her home, but Mister went out to work every day. It had crossed my mind a number of times that it would be a spiritual act of kindness to bake some cookies and take them over for a little visit with Mrs. Wickersham . . . one of these days. It wasn't something I

Holy Assumption of the Virgin Mary Russian Orthodox Church, Kenai, Alaska

looked forward to, so I put the idea out of my mind each time it popped in.

When Mom screamed, Dad jumped up from the chair where he was listening to the radio and ordered me to get the fire extinguisher from the garage. He ran over to the fence and leapt over it like a boy of 16, while I, in my bedroom slippers, ran through the snow to the garage. The long skeleton key hung beside the door, and as I made a grab, it slipped through my cold fingers and dropped into a foot of snow.

Panicked, I prayed, "Please God, let me find it," and thrust my arm into the snow. My hand immediately closed over the key. I threw open the door and grabbed the fire extinguisher off the work bench. When I got to the fence, I could see my father, lying in the snow, his upper half in the trailer door and flames shooting out above him. I tossed the extinguisher to him and he trained it into the tiny trailer. But we were too late. The old lady and the trailer were soon gone. Only a charred frame remained throughout the rest of the winter, reminding me daily that I never baked those cookies for Mrs. Wickersham. It was a bitter lesson. I can only hope that I've partially atoned by other acts of kindness throughout my life.

Maybe I even saved a life one winter soon after. Coming home from school I found a baby in a snowbank. She wasn't a tiny infant but about two years old, shivering in a sweater and sodden diaper. I recognized her, picked her up, wrapped her in my jacket and took her home. There I learned that the parents had gone to spend a few days at their fish site, leaving three little children in the care of a 10-year-old. The baby had toddled away and hadn't been missed yet. That one's for you, Mrs. Wickersham.

Wintertime often brought us some uninvited visitors. When the snow got so deep in the woods that the moose couldn't find food, or they simply got tired of wading around in snow up to their bellybuttons, they headed for town. And then they made their way to the few roads that were cleared. The post office road and our U-shaped driveway were clear. Ergo: We had a moose problem. I'd have to throw sticks at them, or beat on an old pie pan with a spoon, yelling my head off, to get them to move so I could go past, and I wasn't the only one, of course.

Everyone in Kenai was used to dealing with moose. Usually they wouldn't bother you, unless they were harassed by boys with snowballs, or barking dogs. Then they'd put their big, homely heads down, flatten their ears, and start pawing the snow, like *el toro* in a bull ring. The hair on the napes of their necks would rise, as their tongues flicked from side to side. That was your cue to take your pie pan and move on, fast.

A couple of girls were walking to school one day when a moose came charging through the woods after them, several yapping dogs on his heels. The girls began running through the snow but fell over a downed tree—luckily for them. Moose are not normally graceful animals, but this one jumped right over the tree, and the cowering girls, like a steeplechaser. They arrived at school a little soggy and a lot scared, but otherwise unscathed.

Another morning before I was even out of bed, there was a horrendous racket at our door, followed by the sound of someone gasping and stamping his feet in our front room. Mom and Dad were both in the post office, so I cautiously peeked around the corner. There, leaning against our front door, his glasses dangling from one ear, stood our shaken neighbor. Pastor Carl Zehrung, his wife and several children had recently moved into the house next to ours, where they founded the Kenai Church of Christ. They were very good neighbors, but although we lived next to them for years, I don't think I was ever inside their house. Competition for the Kenai Chapel, you know. When I saw Mr. Zehrung panting wild-eyed against our door, I sleepily grunted, "Whaaaa?" and he gasped, "Moose!" "Oh," I said, and turned and went back to bed. I suppose he let himself out when he felt it was safe.

Dad's health slowly improved after we moved to Kenai. Enough so that every year he went moose hunting, usually during moose season. Every year he bagged his moose, which was our main source of meat. Every year I begged to go hunting with him. And just as surely, every year he said, "No."

I felt bad because I, his only child, had turned out to be female. And after all he'd gone through to get me, too. I tried to make up for my gender by volunteering to do guy type stuff with Dad, but obviously it didn't mean the same to him. He almost discouraged me when he muttered how dangerous it was to go tramping through tall grass and maybe step on a bear or something. Almost . . .

Then one year Dad made a concession. Maybe I had grown big

enough, or maybe he was getting older and wearier. At any rate, he promised that after he'd scouted out the territory around his next kill, he'd haul part of the meat home and then take me back to help him bring out the rest. All right! That was more like it: my big opportunity to show him I was every bit as good as any boy-child.

The first day he came back from hunting with no moose. The second day likewise. The third day, still no luck. I was starting to worry. But finally, just after noon on the fourth day, here he came in the pickup, with a quarter of a moose (and the liver, of course) in the back. I hurried into my moose-butchering clothes, and off we drove toward Skilak Lake, one of Dad's favorite hunting areas.

He parked the truck alongside the road, where blood and scraps of moose hair littered the ground, evidence that he'd loaded up there before. We hopped out of the truck and took off at a good pace through the brush. I, of course, struggled manfully (boyfully?) along behind. As I recall, a hunter had to be a half mile off the road to make a legal kill, and there's no telling how many more miles you'd have to search before coming upon a moose willing to be shot.

I was seriously tired and totally lost when we finally arrived at the kill. Not a pretty sight. Dad tossed me a large knife with a curved blade and told me to cut the head off and remove the tongue. He proceeded to butcher the rest of the animal. I could barely budge that huge, shaggy head with its great rack of horns, but I set about whacking away, and after profound effort and much blood, which I sincerely hoped belonged only to the moose, I succeeded in decapitating the beast.

Cutting the tongue out was a moose of a different color. Every so often Dad would glance over and then quickly turn his head and bend to his own task. Once or twice I saw his shoulders shaking, but I assumed he was tiring. I know I was.

By using my hands, both feet and a small log, I was able to hold the moose-mouth open while I stuck my arm down his throat, grasped the enormous tongue and pulled it out as far as it would go. Then I commenced surgery again. Dad had the rest of the moose ready to pack out by the time I finished my labors. I loaded the heart and the tongue on my backpack and we headed for the pickup. He had to make a couple more trips to get the entire moose out, but I'd had

A visitor in Rheingans' yard

Erv Rheingans and a winter's supply of meat

enough guy stuff. We all agreed that the tongue was particularly tasty that year. A bit mangled, but very tasty.

Somehow it was decided that my folks should operate the wireless radio transmitter set when Kenai acquired one. This was to be a public convenience, and I suppose the postmaster's home was the logical location, since everyone came there nearly every day anyway. Also, my folks had to stick fairly close to home because of their post office responsibilities. By then, Dad had sold the fish site and was hired as Mom's second clerk.

Our radio was considered a step up from Mukluk Telegraph, and we felt honored. Someone who wanted to send a telegram would write the message on a pad of paper. The words were carefully counted, payment made, and that night at our appointed time slot of 5:30, Dad or Mom or I would go on the air. Yes, even I.

Lots of times the folks would be busy when our broadcast time arrived, so I'd scoot over to the set, flip a few switches, turn a few dials, and wait breathlessly for our turn. Soon a voice in Anchorage would speak our call letters: "KWJ-3-0 Kenai, KWJ-3-0 Kenai, this is ALB, ALB, ALB Anchorage. Do you read me? Over." Flip switch, press button, and "ALB, ALB, this is KWJ-3-0 Kenai, reading you loud and clear. What have you got for me tonight?" That was great stuff for an 11-year-old.

I learned the phonetic alphabet of that time—Able, Baker, Charlie, Dog—and could spell as phonetically as the next fella. I loved it! Nobody ever questioned my style or complained about my performance. I don't even know if they realized they were dealing with a kid. And people in Kenai seemed confident of my ability as they handed me their carefully thought-out messages.

When I received an incoming message, I'd write it down exactly as received, then type it on yellow paper, "hunt and peck" on our portable typewriter. Finally, if possible, I'd deliver it to the addressee in person. I felt so blamed important. Depending on the urgency of the message, and if I couldn't deliver it on my bike, we sometimes got somebody with a car to take it out to a homestead.

The one negative aspect of our radio set was that the switch (which had to be thrown from right to left or left to right, depending on whether you were receiving or sending) had something wrong with it. Unless you threw the switch with utmost caution, fingers placed precisely on the small Bakelite handle, you would get a shock that would make your hair curl and your toenails turn black. Careful as we all were, it happened just about every time we used the ornery thing. Dad, the original Mr. Fixit, couldn't make it behave, so we finally just learned to grit our teeth and give it the respect it demanded.

While my trusty bike saw plenty of action, I sometimes traveled via stilts. Not, of course, when delivering telegrams. Dad surprised me one day by making me a pair, and I was so touched by his gesture that I risked life and limb to learn to walk on them. The foot supports were only about 18 inches off the ground, but still, you could easily twist your ankle or break your neck on them. We were all surprised when I mastered them, after a fashion.

I very much wanted a motorcycle, but that was out of the question. Somewhere around my 13th year, though, I was able to buy, 10th- or 12th-hand, a Cushman motor scooter. Beat-up and battered, it was beautiful in my eyes, and one of the best investments I ever made. It had a little bean can in back, a trunk-like compartment on which Tuffy loved to ride. His seat was tenuous at best, but he managed to cling to the sloping metal lid, and off we'd roar, with all four of our ears flapping in the breeze. We powered our steed with either gasoline or Blazo kerosene, so naturally I named it Blazo.

At that point I deserted my beloved old bicycle. Blazo became my transportation of choice for the next three years. It was me and Tuffy and Blazo against the world. Look out, world!

10

In the very early 1950s, I received a brown plastic electric radio for Christmas. Since we didn't have electricity, that may seem ridiculous. Actually, it was a declaration of faith, for Kenai was expecting a community power plant, and we intended to be ready for it.

Sure enough, one day I came whistling into the cabin and heard music—not from the front room where the battery-operated Zenith reigned, but from a kitchen shelf: Johnny Ray singing "The Little White Cloud That Cried." Dad was busily stringing wires throughout the house, and before you could say Thomas A. Edison, we had entered the electronic age. No more gas lamps. No more gas irons. No more heating a curling iron on the stove to make those sausage ringlets. Kenai had joined the 20th century.

Of course, Frank Rowley's Kenai Power Company was not the most reliable in the world. Frank tried his best, but we soon grew accustomed to frequent periods of low voltage, when things worked only at half efficiency, as well as out-and-out power failures. It was challenging, but we were grateful.

Also in the early '50s, our new school was built on the outskirts of town, of concrete and steel, with tile floors and acoustical tile ceilings. We eagerly watched its progress and were eventually allowed inside for the Grand Opening. I roamed the wide halls, peeking eagerly into nearly a dozen classrooms, thinking, "This must be what Heaven looks like." Heaven was warm, lit by electricity, and had indoor plumbing and all new desks. It even had an assembly room, which soon doubled as another classroom. We were so proud!

Eighth grade was my first full year in the new school, and although I had had nearly straight A's throughout grade school, for a time it seemed I might not be allowed to graduate. Here's how that happened:

The entire school was preparing for end-of-the-school-year celebrations. The high school kids had their own plan, a trip down the peninsula to Homer, and the rest of us peons were to have a picnic on the schoolground. Everyone was in a festive mood, but some of the

Eighth grade graduates, Kenai Territorial School, 1951: back row, left to right, Roger Tachick, Neil Cole, Pete Petrovich, Gabriel Juliussen, Alec Sacaloff, Alex Ivanoff; front, Betty Cook, Evelyn Baktuit, Bobby Jo Craybaugh, Arlene Rheingans

Mildred Kooly, Leroy Darnell and Evelyn Baktuit at the new school

other eighth-grade girls and I began to feel that as almost-high-schoolers we were too sophisticated for such a mundane activity as a schoolyard picnic. We asked Mr. Connelly, the principal, if we could just bag that day and find our own entertainment.

Mr. C. emphatically vetoed our excellent idea. No amount of pleading moved him; in fact, he vowed dire consequences if we so much as stepped off school property on the day of the picnic.

The six of us were hardly rebels, with or without a cause. But after due consideration, and much heated discussion, we decided to take that step. Ever the dutiful daughter, I did discuss our plans with my mother first. She counseled against crossing Mr. Connelly. But, ever the understanding mother, she eventually left it to me, saying, "You'll have to pay the consequences of your own actions."

Picnic day finally came. Although the snow had melted, and tender shoots of green grass and fresh weeds ventured from the soggy earth, spring's nippy breath still chilled the air, and rain threatened. Undaunted, we young mutineers arrived at school loaded for bear.

As the younger children gathered on the playground for their games and picnic, despite the first sprinkles of rain, we crept away into the woods, thrilled at our own derring-do. Down the trail to Beaver Dam we ran, giggling and dodging mud puddles and soggy foliage. In winter Beaver Dam was a favorite skating rink, as it was both a pond and a creek. When the water froze hard enough to support a Jeep, to clear off the snow, we spent many happy hours gliding over the ice.

On this day, however, Beaver Dam pond was a murky brown pool. But to us it could have been Lake Como, and we could have been in sunny Italy instead of wiping rivulets of Alaskan rain off the ends of our noses.

Our first order of business was to find some dry twigs to start a fire. That took the better part of an hour. By then we were thoroughly soaked but eagerly anticipating lunch. It turned out that baking raw potatoes in a pitiful campfire took longer than we cared to wait, so we opened a large can of beans and set it carefully beside the fire to heat. Beans and potatoes being our entire bill of fare, we were too eager to wait long. With the chill barely off the beans, we prepared to start feasting—until we realized we had no plates or utensils.

Not to worry. Were we not Alaskans? Were we not used to difficult circumstances? Were we not starving? You bet! As several of us had brought pocketknives, we soon whittled makeshift spoons and dug into the bean can.

At this point a rustling in the bushes disturbed our banquet, and Mr. Connelly and Mildred's father burst upon the scene. Mr. C. was outraged, but Milly's dad took one look at us six drowned rats, huddled around our pathetic fire, digging with sticks into a can of lukewarm beans, and he began to laugh. His laughter did not improve Mr. C.'s disposition.

Milly's dad turned around and, still roaring with laughter, made his way back home, leaving us to the wrath of Mr. Connelly. We were promptly marched back to school, where we were told we would not be graduating.

Well, there was quite a stink about that decision. Several of the parents, my mother included, felt the punishment was too severe for the crime. They prevailed upon Mr. C. to reduce his sentence to merely giving us F's in deportment, and we were allowed to graduate. I thought it was mighty big of Mom to stick up for us after saying we'd have to bear the consequences of our actions. I believe she thought that the scare was bad enough, and that having an "F" on my pristine report card was probably as much pain as I could stand. What a mother!

Since there were only eight kids in our graduating class, it wasn't too difficult to be valedictorian. However, it was with a certain amount of pride that I gave my commencement address, reprinted here for the edification of posterity:

Always Room at the Top

By Arlene M. Rheingans

Parents, teachers and friends. We of the 8th grade wish to welcome you to our graduation exercises and are glad that you can share with us this happiness.

We wish to thank our parents for getting us up and sending us to school. We wish to thank all our teachers whether here or not, for their understanding and patience which were both given to us in great abundance. And also, we wish to thank all our friends, the taxpayers, for helping us to have this beautiful school, the projector, the playground equipment and all the other things which make going to school more pleasant and enjoyable for us.

Education is the way through which a person develops his abilities, attitudes and general behavior. Through education at the Kenai school, all of us have developed abilities. To some extent, we have all learned to read, spell, write, etc. Also, we have learned how to try to get along with our fellow students and teachers.

I hope that all of our attitudes have been changed since we were of preschool age. Our outlook on life is surely brighter now that we know what others are talking about and now that we know how to do things and can be a part of the community. The last point on this definition of education is our general behavior. I'm afraid to make a point on that so I shall leave that up to you teachers, parents and friends. [Pause for laugh.] However, here is something that I think we would all be better off if we followed:

> There was an old owl who lived in an oak
> The more he saw the less he spoke.
> The less he spoke the more he heard.
> Why can't we all be like that old bird?

Since we students are going to take over what you have started and carry out the policies you have adopted to the control of our cities, states and nation, and since we are going to move in and take over churches, schools and corporations, the fate of humanity is in our hands. We realize how important education will be to accomplish all this.

In closing, I would like to leave this poem (author unknown) to my fellow graduates to encourage them to get all the education they can:

> Never you mind the crowd, lad,
> Nor fancy your life won't tell.
> The work is the work for all that
> To him that doeth it well.

Fancy the world a hill, lad,
Look where the millions stop.
You'll find the crowd at the base, lad.
But there's always room at the top.
Courage and faith and patience –
There's space in this old world yet.
The better chance you'll find, lad,
The farther along you get.
Keep your eye on the goal, lad.
Never despair nor drop.
Be sure that your path points upward.
There's always room at the top!!

And now I'm sure that you will all join with me in hoping that four years from now you will see each one of us getting our high school diplomas.

Oh my. As it turned out, I did graduate from high school. But not with those kids, and not from Kenai Territorial School.

We had such a good time in that new building! Because we finally had an auditorium large enough to accommodate most of the townspeople, we held frequent programs and plays. I still loved performing, although there were moments that caused me to scrap any serious plans of becoming a thespian.

As one of four "End Men" (Evelyn and I were End Women) for a minstrel show one year, I was dressed in a long, oversized dress and apron, stuffed front and back with pillows that kept slipping down before the curtain went up. Worried that I'd lose voluptuousness mid-performance, I found several large safety pins and fastened the pillows to my underpants. The problem was solved—until I did my dance number. Then, twirling and bopping, I felt an ominous slippage. Both my hands were holding a broom, so I couldn't prevent pillows AND underpants from dropping to the stage. Like a trooper, I kicked the pile off stage and continued my dance a much thinner and more risque End Person.

When the high school performed "Tom Sawyer," I was Aunt Polly. I would have preferred Becky Thatcher, since she was the romantic lead, but because I was half a head taller than any of the boys, I was Aunt Polly. I told myself it was a more challenging part than Becky

Kenai Territorial School, 1948

KENAI TERRITORIAL SCHOOL ~ ELEMENTARY AND HIGH SCHOOL

K-1848-53   K.C.L.A

The new school, early 1950s

since Aunt Polly required a considerable amount of aging: special make-up, powder in the hair, a more mature voice. A real stretch for my talents. Opening night was a mad cycle of frequent dashes down the hall to the girls' rest room and long gulps from the water fountain on the way back, to ease my parched throat. Two minutes till show time, I *knew* my bladder was going to fail me. I flew down the hall, Aunt Polly's skirts whirling around my ankles, charged into the rest room stall, and slammed the door behind me. Up went the long ruffled skirt, down went the panties, and whewwww, what a relief. Except that somebody had left the toilet lid down. Aunt Polly performed with damp skirts and soggy shoes.

We had the greatest time with those plays. Everyone pitched in to make scenery, design and sew costumes, gather props, or provide special sound effects. Our efforts were always rewarded with much applause and many thumbs up by our appreciative, entertainment-starved audiences. We were always a HIT!

Some of the plays I remember best: "Snowbound For Christmas" (in which the cast wore pj's and nighties for one of the acts, and I felt quite daring in a new yellow brushed-flannel gown); "Christmas in Toyland" (I was Nurse Sunshine); "The Phantom Strikes Again" (in which I actually kissed the leading man, a boy named Roger who probably dreaded the smooch as much as I did); and "Dangerous Ambrose."

Regarding the last, though I can't for the life of me remember my role, I do know that several of us had to recite: "Why, he's a pragmatic prevaricator with a propensity for oratorical sonorosity which is too pleonastic to be expeditiously assimilated." I'll never forget that line, nor the one that follows: "In other words, he's a hot-air shooter!"

Occasionally we held talent shows. Usually the acts consisted of singing, a bit of acrobatics, a poetic recital, and a musical instrument solo. Once we were treated to a baton-twirling demonstration.

Then there moved to town a girl who played the accordion, so of course she was drafted for our next talent night. A few days before the program, she came down with the mumps. Our teacher, greatly disappointed, asked without any real hope if anybody else could play the accordion. Hesitating not a moment, I raised my hand. Teacher was thrilled; I was stunned. Displaying more bravado than sense, I borrowed the afflicted girl's squeezebox and practiced frantically. The

Mildred Kooly, Jean Stock, Barbara Sandstrom, Jerry Benson, Kathleen Reger, Carol Jones (obscured), Dorothy Sandstrom

*From left: Judy (or Nancy) Kent, Evelyn Baktuit,
Edna Monfor and Arlene in "Tom Sawyer"*

Nathan Bagley as The Inspector in "The Phantom Strikes Again"

simplest song in the history of music, with the possible exception of "I Am Playing Middle C," has to be "Silent Night," so that's what I played at the program. You guessed it: I was a HIT! Every entertainer should have Kenai audiences.

As I've said, I loved to sing. I was no Mrs. Munson, but then, who was? Pavarotti is no Mrs. Munson. Once I'd mastered harmony, I much preferred having someone else take the lead, but I'd attempt most anything. Twice I sang a solo at weddings in the Chapel: "Because God Made Thee Mine," and "O Promise Me."

One Christmas a handsome young fellow named Leroy and I had roles in our Sunday School play. He was a great guy, an only child like me, whose father worked for the Road Commission. We were friends, always teasing and joking. The day of our dress rehearsal, as we left the Chapel, Leroy watched me pick my way along the icy walkway. "I hope you break your leg," he teased, and I yelled right back, "I hope you break your neck." We both laughed. Those were the last words I exchanged with my friend Leroy.

That evening we all waited backstage at the Chapel. Leroy was late. The congregation became restless. Finally, the other classes did their pieces, and then a note arrived. The missionary read the message silently and then stepped to the pulpit and announced: "There will be no Christmas play tonight."

As the congregation filed out, we were told that Leroy had killed himself with his own rifle. A friend of ours had stopped to bring him to town and found his body. Many people in Kenai thought Leroy had committed suicide, but we'll never know.

Now, after nearly 50 years, I remember exactly how I felt that night. I knew I'd never be able to think, much less talk, about Leroy without tears. It still hurts. I think it always will.

Not too long after electricity arrived, my folks decided to build a new house. This undertaking was carried out solely by my father, with a little help from me, and took several years. Not only did he design the place, a two-bedroom, one-bath frame house on a full cement basement, but he ordered everything except the lumber from Outside. And he and Mom paid for it as he went along. The materials came, project by project, via the Alaska Steamship Company to Seward. Then Dad had to haul them to Kenai in the pickup. Bad roads and bad weather caused delays. Shipping strikes held things up. When some construction problem stumped him, Dad would calmly sit in his big chair, listen to quiet music on the old Zenith, and think about it. He'd think and think until Mom was ready to scream, but only when he had mentally solved the problem to his absolute satisfaction would he attempt the actual solution. This process sometimes took a week or two. The new house was, therefore, a labor of love *and* frustration.

Dad did hire a "catskinner" to excavate the full basement, and a well digger to dig the well. Then he built and set the forms for the full basement, got hold of a cement mixer, and the two of us began hauling gravel and mixing. Dad did the really hard work. I stood on the 10-foot wall forms on a little catwalk and tamped the cement firmly into the forms with an oar-like tool. He was a real bear about getting the cement "tight" with no air holes or cracks. It was terrifically hard work, and we were both delighted and a little surprised when the day finally came to remove the forms and our finished product turned out not only tight but smooth as a baby's hind end.

I got fairly good with the hammer and nails but probably didn't do as much as I'd like to think I did. I never could saw a straight line.

When Dad got the 2 x 4s up inside and outside the house, he let the rest go and concentrated on the bathroom. It was gorgeous: green tile on walls and floor, sink and tub with hot and cold running water, a flush toilet, the whole shootin' match. We could finally dispense with the outdoor privy and the round galvanized bathtub. During the months and years it took to complete the rest of the house, we luxuriated in that bathroom.

Postal patrons would greet us on Saturday evenings as, one after another, we trotted in our bathrobes from the old cabin to the skeletal new house, towels and soap in hand, anticipating our weekly soak in the gleaming porcelain fixture. For some time the house had no walls except for the bathroom, which was substantially enclosed and had a door that locked. Anyplace but Kenai, our bathing routine might have seemed eccentric, but in Kenai, nobody batted an eyelash.

Regarding bathing in general: In my opinion, it's overdone these days. Too many people insist on a daily or even twice-daily "cleansing." They hop into and out of a wimpy little stream of tepid water and consider that an ablution. But it's well known that too much soap and water is harmful to the skin, not only washing away natural body oils but often leaving behind a film of soap residue to clog the pores.

Erv and Joyce Rheingans in the new house

"Big brother" Bobby Tachick

Teacher David Duddles—here with wife Beth and daughter Gayle—directed many of the high school productions.

It seems to me that a couple or three good soaks and scrubs a week should suffice. Specific body parts requiring special attention can be dealt with daily, but why punish the body's largest organ by daily soap-and-watering it? Do you really need dry, wrinkly skin? I don't think so.

One day while Dad and I were putting up sheetrock, a group of rowdy fishermen came to collect their mail. These weren't local men, but fellows from Puget Sound who fished Alaskan waters in drift boats during the season. Kenai people, who fished from beach sites, resented the "foreigners" with their huge gill nets capturing the bulk of the salmon. The "Pewgie Islanders" didn't like the Kenai folk either, so there were brawls aplenty when the two factions met.

On this particular day, Dad and I were working obscured behind the sheetrock as the fishermen ripped into their mail. They stood just the other side of the wall, loudly and profanely discussing their letters and the "girls they left behind." The air was blue. Dad set down his hammer, stuck his head out the window opening, and said in the most quiet, deadly voice: "Watch your language, men, there's a lady present." Without a word, the men left. I nearly keeled over with pleased surprise. I've never been prouder of my dad than I was at that moment. Maybe he didn't come to my graduation or attend the plays and programs I appeared in, but when the chips were down, he was my hero.

Around this time I attracted an ardent admirer named Richard, a newcomer to Kenai who was several years older than I. He was cute, with curly brown hair, long-lashed eyes, and access to his father's car. And to top it off, he could play the guitar and sing like Hank Snow. Sounds like a perfect beau for me, but although I liked him, I had my sights set on other game at the time.

Richard was seriously smitten, though, and he was a most persistent Romeo. For several years he was my shadow; sometimes I'd deign to notice him and allow him to drive me around in his dad's car, and sometimes I'd even let him serenade me, but usually I just tried to ignore him.

Richard unnerved my folks by parking his dad's car right in front of our kitchen window and then sitting on the hood, staring at us as we ate our meals. Sometimes he'd be there when we went to bed at night, and there when we got up in the morning. I was both flattered and annoyed, but there was no discouraging Richard, who was nothing if not steadfast.

Like most 13-year-old girls, I had a selfish streak, and I wasn't above using Richard when I needed a favor or an errand run. I'm not proud of that. When I determined to learn to drive, who better to teach me than Richard? One summer evening we picked up a couple of other girls and set off for a drive out Beaver Loop Road. Richard had already given me a few driving lessons, so when we got out of town four or five miles, I suggested he play the guitar and I take the wheel. Against his better judgment, but unable to refuse me anything, Richard changed seats with me and off we lurched.

We were tooling along, singing "Bluebird Island," when we came to a stretch of road covered in deeper than usual gravel. Richard suggested that I gear down, and I expertly threw the gearshift—not into second, but reverse. The next sound we heard was the transmission making violent protest.

We were deep in bear country, and it was nighttime, but there was nothing for us to do but set off walking toward town. Now and then a tree would rub against another, producing an eerie, screeching sound. Richard carried his guitar, and we all held hands, but we didn't feel like singing anymore. No cars came by for a few miles until finally Walt Christensen, bringing the boat mail from Seward in his truck, drew up and gave us a lift. I wonder if Richard told his dad who was responsible for the ruined transmission. I seriously doubt it. He was too gallant.

Thirty-some years later I went back to Kenai and looked Richard up. He had married a lovely girl from Utah and was about to become a grandfather. I enjoyed seeing him again, but I confess it was a little sad no longer to be the object of such adoration.

Another great friend of the opposite sex was Bobby Tachick, who was like a big brother, someone you loved to pal around with and could always count on. When I came down with the mumps, after he'd joined the Army, he came to visit me, risking the same fate for himself. I had lots of friends, but only a few really close ones, and I never dated any of the local boys I grew up with. A few of them were "boyfriends" when I was a kid, but once I got to high school, they didn't interest me that way.

However, I acquired another best friend. We'd known each other since I was in the third grade but seemed to have absolutely nothing in common until I was in high school. Her name was Jackie Benson; she was 2½ years older than I (still is), and we became pals.

Jackie and I began spending most waking hours together, and some sleeping hours, too. Her dad was boss of the Alaska Road Commission gang, so she lived at the ARC camp a few miles from Kenai. We'd walk, run, ride bikes and/or Blazo, whatever it took to be together. I felt I'd found somebody who shared my sense of the outlandish, and who inspired me to push myself a bit.

Jackie was bright. (Still is.) She kept me on my toes. (Still does.) She was well-read by Kenai standards, so in order to hold my own with her, I had to become better-read myself. She played the piano better than I; I practiced harder so we could play duets together. We wowed 'em at the Kenai Chapel with our rendition of "Onward Christian Soldiers." Such passion, such speed, such deployment of the loud pedal!

Jackie had very long hair which she wore in a queue down her back, so I let my hair grow long, too. I never attempted the pigtail, however. It just wasn't me. But it was (and is) Jackie.

My new friend had a passion for long, full, gathered skirts, and seemed to have an endless supply of them. Every weekend she'd show up in a new one. This puzzled me, until I learned that she made them herself. She showed me how to gather a long length of fabric onto a waistband, hem the bottom and sew a zipper up the back. We were a little shaky on the zippers, but to this day the gathered full skirt is my favorite homemade fashion. Oh sure, I've made western shirts, tailored pants, a formal or two, several dozen children's dresses and more Halloween costumes than I care to remember. But I really shine at the full gathered skirt, thanks to Jackie.

When she started coming to the Kenai Chapel, I began enjoying my religion more. We taught Sunday School and Daily Vacation Bible School together—the preschool class, 10 or so 3-, 4- and 5-year-olds in a small room in the church basement. Besides a low table and a dozen munchkin-sized chairs, we had an ancient, asthmatic, foot-pumped organ that had only a few keys missing, and whose various control knobs we never even tried to understand. Jackie usu-

At "Da Bank"—Edward Segura, Arlene, Evelyn Baktuit

*Hap (right), Chick and Blazo (someone should have told
Chick that the kickstand was still down)*

ally performed at the organ, while I led the singing. We had a pretty tuneful little group, with the possible exception of Joyce T., a tiny blonde who was a monotone of the first caliber and always sang (loudly and in a very deep voice) one or two notes behind everybody else: "Jesus loves me, this I know (I know) . . ." I was fascinating at the flannelboard; Jackie excelled during the artsy-craftsy period. We both felt very maternal.

I don't think it was Jackie's influence but rather the fact that I was 13 and going through a mildly rebellious stage that caused me to participate in bouts of mildly rebellious behavior. Who actually proposed our little flights of flimflam is anybody's guess at this date; let's say it was mutual.

One fine day we went to Anchorage with Jimmy and Evelyn Petersen, who had business there and left us to our own, surely trustworthy, devices. After much fascinated window shopping—real stores, not the Kenai Commercial or Casey Jones' grocery—we happened upon the movie theater, where Dean Martin and Jerry Lewis were appearing in that timeless classic *Jumping Jacks.* Even knowing that one step inside was surefire heck and darnation didn't slow us down. In we strode, bought bags of popcorn and settled down to howl along with Dean and Jerry. When we emerged, limp from laughing, we decided to rename ourselves after the *Jumping Jacks* characters: Jackie became Chick, Dean's alter ego, and I became Hap—the goofy one, of course. From that day on, we were Chick and Hap. (Still are.)

Blissfully unaware that we'd been observed coming out of the theater (gasp!), we meandered across the street to the Federal Building where a bored news peddler stood unsuccessfully pushing that day's paper. We offered to increase his sales. Ignoring his doubtful shrug, we each grabbed an armload of newspapers and stood on the steps of the Federal Building yodeling in our best Hank Williams style: "If you've got the money, we've got The Ti-i-imes . . ." We sold all our papers and got a few interesting comments in the bargain, most of which we didn't understand.

We weren't in Anchorage more than a few hours, so we couldn't get into too much trouble. But trouble caught up with me when I got back home. Early the next day the missionary's wife arrived at our house to read me the riot act. Seems she had been in Anchorage the day before, walking down Fourth Avenue, when who should she see coming out of the movie theater but her two Sunday School teachers, ol' "Hap and Chick." I listened respectfully but with an unrepentant heart, mostly grateful that she hadn't seen us peddling our papers.

On nights when our folks would let us "sleep over" at each other's homes, we'd crawl into whoever's small bed we were sharing that night, pull the covers over our heads, and by flashlight read such mind-expanding tomes as we could get our hands on. Max Shulman's *Barefoot Boy With Cheek, The Feather Merchants* and *Rally 'Round The Flag, Boys* sent us near hysteria. Of course, they had about as much educational value as *Jumping Jacks* (or my children's *Gilligan's Island*), but we thought Max was terrific. One line sticks in my head: "Hubba hubba, Goodrich rubba." No wonder we had two of the highest IQs tested at Kenai Territorial School in our era. I recently ran across Mr. Shulman's *Anyone Got a Match* and found it not a bit funny. Just wasn't the same without Chick and the flashlight.

We read somewhere that a person could get drunk by combining aspirin with Coca Cola. Neither aspirin nor soft drinks were prohibited by Kenai Chapel, but we had to give it a go anyway.

A grand lady named Louisa Miller was operating Kenai's first soda fountain, near Da Bank between our house and the Chapel. Louisa made the very first pizza I ever tasted, but it was foreign to our palates and none of us liked it, so she took it off the menu. That's really hard to believe now, when pizza ranks right up there with lobster in my book. Louisa sometimes allowed Chick and me to "soda jerk"—shades of Archie and Veronica and the Sweet Shoppe! We even made some tips, though we'd gladly have paid her for the privilege of being part of the action.

For our daring experiment, Chick and I bought a bottle of aspirin at Kenai Commercial and headed over to Mrs. Miller's place, where we ordered two bottles of Coke, ensconced ourselves in the back booth and set about crushing aspirin as best we could and funneling it into the bottles. We sipped hesitantly at first, sure that the concoction was going to take immediate effect, then, disillusioned but still a bit apprehensive, drained the drinks just as Louisa's husband, Freddie, approached to ask with a frown, "You kids aren't up to something, are you?" "Uhhh, no," we blurted, and fled, leaving behind twin bottles coated with aspirin residue. Freddie, who owned and operated a bar on the edge of town, undoubtedly recognized suspicious characters when he saw them. The experiment didn't make us drunk, but it probably did irreparable damage to our kidneys or livers or whatever. On the bright side, I never had a headache for the rest of high school, either.

I suppose we were a little preoccupied with forbidden fruits just then, because not long after that episode, we decided to get the whole Kenai Chapel Youth Fellowship tipsy.

Most of the young people in town enjoyed the Friday night KYF, and meetings were quite well attended. We met for a couple of hours in the church basement for games, then went up to the sanctuary for an hour of singing and preaching, and then back downstairs for refreshments, usually cake or cookies and fruit punch.

At that time the Army had stationed a very small contingent of men near Kenai, and the local girls were delighted when some of the young fellows started coming to dances and to the Chapel. No doubt the soldiers, many of them still teenagers themselves, were as interested in meeting girls as they were in hearing the gospel, but nevertheless, they came. The Kenai boys were disgusted.

Chick and I coaxed one of the GIs into buying a half-pint of vodka (representing about as much tip money as we had amassed), which we hid in a pocket until KYF refreshment time. Then we surreptitiously poured the vodka into the punch. I say "we" because I don't remember which of us did the dastardly deed. Chick now insists we were too self-righteous to drink any ourselves, but I don't remember it that way. (Stark terror does funny things to the memory; so does the march of time.) However, I do remember one of the female pillars of the church, who was acting as chaperone, smacking her lips and pronouncing loudly, "This is the best punch I've ever tasted!" as she poured her third glassful.

Chick and I were concerned that we might not know how to kiss properly—or improperly, depending on your viewpoint—if the occasion should ever arise. I recall riding in the back of a pickup truck, the wind whipping our hair into our eyes, solemnly discussing the intricacies of "the smooch." We debated the pros and cons of wetting the lips first, and of opening the mouth ever so slightly. I suggested that, in the interest of scientific research, we kiss each other and then be perfectly frank in critiquing one another's performance. Chick was doubtful but reluctantly agreed. We gritted our teeth and drew closer together, staring determinedly into each other's eyes. When our noses were about two inches apart, we burst out laughing and that was the end of another Great Experiment.

One thing that really bugged me about Chick was her dawdling. When she stayed at my house, Mom would wake us up for school, and then my agony would begin. I'd brush my teeth, comb my hair, get dressed, eat breakfast and be ready to leave, while Chick was still standing there, brushing her teeth. With a rapt, thoughtful expression, she stared at the wall as if watching a movie. Back and forth, up and down, over and over ad infinitum, she scrubbed, while I hopped from one foot to the other, threatening dire things if she didn't get a move on. I had a fetish about being late, so a few times I gave up in disgust and walked to school alone. That didn't faze Chick . . . brush, brush, back and forth, up and down. I don't know whether she was late or not, as we were in different classes.

On days we didn't have to rush off to school (or not rush, in Chick's case), we'd make our favorite breakfast: huge cups of hot cocoa and easily a loaf of bread, toasted slice by slice and spread with chunky peanut butter. Of course, that was in the days when our tummies were concave instead of convex. Sigh.

The old Kenai Territorial School, late 1948 (page 189): From the front row, left, and reading back and forth to the back row: (1, from left) Vivian Juliussen, Sigrid Juliussen, Sharon Wright, Carol Baktuit, Judy Juliussen, Virginia Monfor, Skip White, Charlie House, Alec Wik, Victor Segura, Jimmy Sanders, Harriet Mann, Jeanette Thornton, Ernie Jordan, Virginia Hunter; (2, from right) Harry House, Rudy Wilson, Jimmy Segura, Glen Kooly, Jerry Benson, Nels Juliussen (cap over eyes), Jacob Titus, unidentified brother and sister, Violet Sanders, Carol Jones, unidentified (Tommy ?), Freda Monfor, Mott Fuller, Gabe Juliussen, Alfred Ivanoff, Jeanie Onkka;

(3, from left) Arlene Rheingans, Evelyn Baktuit, Neil Cole, Roy Soper, Mildred Kooly, Vernon Petterson, George Hunter, Charlotte March, Alex Sacaloff, Lena Titus; (4, from right) Edna Monfor, Don Cole, Jackie Benson, Marie Sanders, Leona March, Joyce Wilson, Alice Ness, Alex Ivanoff, Leroy Darnell, Bill Wright; (5, from left) Anne Lewis, Joann Kooly, Alida Petterson, Anna Ivanoff, Odman Kooly, Albert Baktuit, Dona Soper, Carl Petterson; (6, from right) Gordon Baktuit, Sam Holstrom, Bobby Lemmon, Bob Mamaloff, Eddie Ness, Chuck Lewis, Nick Mamaloff, Irene Ness. Teachers, top row from left, are Peggy Petersen Arness, teaching principal O.C. Connelly, Ruth Connelly and Jettie Petersen.

11

EVEN BEFORE THE MILITARY INSTALLED its little bases at Kenai, first at the airstrip out toward the ARC camp and then a larger one at Wildwood Station, out the north road, they stationed three lonely airmen out in the boondocks on the far side of Skilak Lake. This was maybe 20 miles from town, and on or near the Kenai Moose Range. Why Uncle Sam would need three GIs out there, I didn't know then and I sure don't know now, but perhaps the moose felt more secure. The senior member of the trio, one Art F., rarely came to town. Johnny D., a younger, friendly, dark-haired fellow from Pensylvania, made as many trips to town as possible, for any excuse he could think of. Especially after he started dating Chick.

I use the term "dating" loosely, for there wasn't that much to do on a date in Kenai, but they did start to look seriously smitten. Chick prevailed upon Johnny to bring the third member of their troop to town to meet her pal Hap. This fellow was a young blond from Oklahoma with the intriguing name of Valjean Skaggs. He used quaint expressions like "pully-bone" for wishbone, and I thought he looked a lot like Alan Ladd. What he thought of escorting a 13-year-old around is anybody's guess; at any rate, it didn't last long. Either he preferred to hide out on the far side of Skilak Lake with the moose, or he was transferred to greener ranges, for he disappeared from my life as suddenly as he arrived.

Shortly after that, Uncle Sam established the Air Force camp out by the airstrip, and I began "dating" some of those fellows. That is to say, they arrived at my house and went to church activities with me, and sometimes had a meal with my family. The first was a cute little fellow from the Dakotas named Leonard; the second was a bit taller and named Harlen. Both were medics, Harlen succeeding Leonard both at the base and in my heart. Alas, both of them also were transferred elsewhere all too soon.

The little encampment out by the airfield was soon closed permanently, and a larger contingent of Army troops was brought to Wildwood Station. At this juncture the Kenai girls thought their prayers had been answered. During the next few years, most of the girls my age and older married those soldiers.

Chick escaped. She graduated from high school very young and left for business college in Seattle in the fall of 1953. After finishing business school, she took a job working for a judge in Anchorage and we rarely saw each other anymore. I missed her a great deal, and looked for ways to keep busy.

The "dating game" was the only game in town, except for the Chapel functions. After several false starts, I began going steady with a young soldier from Georgia, a Korean War veteran named Walter Hotchkiss. He was seven years older than I and my folks were less then thrilled about the relationship, but eventually they accepted what seemed inevitable.

Walter and I settled into being a couple. He was personable and fun to be with, but I was warned by several people that he was untruthful and not right for me. Unfortunately, I didn't listen. When I was 14½, we became officially engaged.

Around 1952, a squadron of the Civil Air Patrol had been formed in Kenai, and both Walter and I eventually joined the active cadet squadron, made up of young people eager to learn to fly, though somewhat less eager to rescue downed bush pilots should the need arise. We met on the school grounds and learned to salute, march, obey marching commands ("Squadron, about face, harch; squadron, left face, harch; squadron, right face, har— that's *right* face, cadets, *right* face. One rock, knuckleheads, one rock!"), and eventually we took first aid classes and even some flying lessons. An ancient Linc Trainer found its way to us, and then the fun really began.

A few of us even bought CAP uniforms. It was a proud day when I, in blue and white skirt, blouse and cap, received my promotion to second lieutenant and cadet adjutant.

Although I'm sure the CAP has been instrumental in rescuing a number of pilots, I never had the privilege. I did take part in a mock rescue. One of our commanders landed his small plane on a lake and then we, riding shotgun with another commander, had to seek and find him and his cadet companion, bind up their "wounds" and evacuate them. Since we had only two search planes and each plane held only one cadet passenger, it took forever for the whole squadron to take turns finding the crash site. Consequently, the "downed pilot"

2nd Lt. Arlene, Civil Air Patrol

Visiting cousins Denny and Christine Randleman

and his passenger nearly froze to death before we all finally got there to rescue them.

Besides acquiring a fiance, it was during this time that I finally gained some bona fide, on-the-scene relatives. Until then, with the exception of Uncle Willy, my young godfather, none of our family had ever come to Alaska. Whereas just about everyone I knew had sisters and/or brothers, myriad aunts, uncles, cousins and grandparents, our family was Just We Three.

Dad's younger sister, my Aunt Alice, called Leets, and her husband, Corwin, had decided to move to Alaska. With them they brought my two cousins. Denny was around 10 or 11, and baby Christine was just learning to walk. Although much of my time and interest were taken with Walter, I was delighted to have this extended family, who moved into our old cabin, directly behind the new house.

Christine was too small to be much of a pal, but she was a cute little bundle, and I loved helping my aunt take care of her. Denny became the little brother I'd never had. He and I had a great time exploring Kenai. We roamed the beach; we slept in the back yard in sleeping bags and a pup tent, and we decided to go digging for Indian artifacts.

For some reason we thought there might be something of interest along the bank over on the CAA land. I knew we weren't supposed to mess around on government property, but Denny's enthusiasm overcame my better judgment. Off we sped on Blazo, Denny with the shovels over his shoulder and me at the controls.

We were digging away in the tall grass, in which we hoped to find signs of ancient Indian ruins, when I glanced up and saw one of the government men coming toward us. I panicked. Fearing we'd be arrested, I whispered to Denny, "Quick, run!" and we grabbed our shovels and skedaddled. Crouching low in the grass and weeds, we snuck back to the road, hopped on Blazo and blazed out of there.

However, I wasn't about to get off that easily. The CAA man had seen Blazo and recognized it as belonging to the postmaster's daughter. Never mind about being on government property. Never mind digging up Indian burial treasures. This fellow had a nasty mind, and he proceeded straight to the post office to inform Mom that her daughter had been "taking advantage of a little boy!"

Since Den and I had just minutes before come home in a lather and confessed our trespassing to both our mothers, Mom was as indignant at that fellow as he was at me. She told him off, and for once the story didn't make the rounds of Kenai. A minor miracle. I was thoroughly embarrassed, though, and lived for a while in agony that the town would hear the trumped-up tale. I guess Mom made a believer out of that jerk.

It was a shame, though, for I never felt comfortable running around with my little cousin after that. In any case, their family didn't stay in Alaska very long. Work was hard to find and little Christine required medical attention, so our relatives soon returned to Minnesota.

A year or two later, the Schmidt family, Alvin and Evie, their two children and Evie's parents, who were Dad's cousins, drove over the Alcan Highway to spend a week with us. Although they were my second, third and fourth cousins, it was great fun to have relatives around again, even for so short a time. I remembered how much fun I'd had staying with Alvin and Evie on their farm years before, while Dad had his operations.

I think a person misses out on a lot of good times and joy without relatives close at hand. Of course, maybe you miss a lot of aggravation and grief, too, so I suppose it evens out.

Another embarrassing thing happened during this period. One day Mom asked me to take some clothes to the dry cleaner (yes, Kenai had acquired a dry cleaning establishment) out the north road toward Wildwood Station. As it was only a mile or so from town, I didn't mind the walk. Coming back, on a lonely stretch of road between the dry cleaner and Kenai's first buildings, I heard a voice call, "Hey, honey," from the woods to my right and slightly behind me. I turned to see who had called, and standing there, amid the fireweed and grass, was a man with his T-shirt pulled up over his head. Other than that, he was naked as a jaybird, beckoning with his hand and another appendage to come over and join him.

After one brief but mortified look, I turned and made for home as fast as my dignity would permit. I knew I couldn't outrun him if it came down to it, and I also didn't want to give him the satisfaction of seeing that he'd upset me. I walked as fast as I could, hoping and praying with all my might. Oddly, I wasn't afraid of the man. I was more afraid that a car would come along and see both me and him and make a disgusting connection. That is, my terror of "what Kenai might think" was much greater than any fear for my own safety. A depressing indictment of small-town living.

When I appeared back home, Mom immediately sensed that something was wrong. I at first insisted not, but she kept at me, and I finally, much humiliated, admitted what had happened. She indignantly accompanied me to Marshal Petersen's, where I had to tell my story again, and the marshal and some other men went out to the spot I showed them. Of course the pervert was already gone, but they found the grass beaten down and many cigarette butts where he'd been standing.

Some time later he pulled his nasty stunt on two little girls in the old school building in the heart of town. They yelled bloody murder, and the man was caught and put in jail. Where, it is hoped, he was treated with the same respect he showed women and girls.

When Walter was eligible to be discharged from the Army, he chose to remain in Alaska instead of mustering out in the States. He didn't even go home for a visit but took a civilian job working on the base and waited for me to be old enough to wed.

We were married 12 days after my 16th birthday, with my parents' consent if not their enthusiasm, and only after my solemn promise to finish my last year of high school and get my diploma. Early marriages weren't unusual in Kenai, and I wasn't the first or only married woman to attend high school there. It was a formal wedding, and very nice. We set up housekeeping in a small, old trailer house near Wildwood.

Just a few months after the wedding, Dad was invited by Jimmy Petersen to go moose hunting with him. They were best friends, as I said, and often hunted together, and Dad surely would have gone that time except that he had a terrible head cold and didn't think he could keep up with Jimmy, who was about 20 years younger than he. "If you don't get your moose tomorrow, I'll go with you in a day or two," he promised Jimmy.

But the next day, word came to us that Jimmy and the fellow who went in Dad's place hadn't come home that night. They didn't come home the next night, either. Jimmy's wife contacted her father-in-law, and Marshal Petersen and a group of other men, Dad and Walter included, headed out to the Skilak Lake area where Jimmy had said he was going to hunt.

Thus began two weeks of searching, hoping, praying, and finally, resignation and sorrow. We women made sandwiches and coffee and set up a small refreshment camp on the lake shore, while the ever-growing search party combed the lake and the surrounding area. Some Fish and Wildlife oil cans were found, along with a few bits of equip-ment, and a fresh kill was located that looked like Jimmy's work. Other than that, nothing was found. The boat, the men—everything had disappeared.

As the search ended, returning to my parents' home I found my father weeping. I'd never seen Dad cry, and it had a profound effect on me. I saw, perhaps for the first time, that he felt deeply about some people. I was surprised and touched. A few months later, when Walter and I left to live in Georgia, I again saw tears in my father's eyes. It was both gratifying and sorrowful to me, for I wished he could have shown more emotion and affection during my childhood, and not waited until I was leaving.

Kenai, Alaska, June 17, 1955

Outside

12

*I*T WAS MARCH OF 1956 AND I had started to think about graduation when Walter decided he wanted to go home. Right now. Although I was to have been valedictorian of my class, and as such had been offered a scholarship to the University of Alaska (which I wouldn't have accepted), we set off for Savannah, Georgia.

It was hard leaving my folks and friends, but I wasn't sorry to bid Kenai farewell. For a long time I'd been eager to escape the small town life-in-a-goldfish-bowl. Reading *Life* and *Look* and *Saturday Evening Post* had made me want to experience a lot more than Kenai had to offer, and those movie mags and Archie comics had given me glamorized expectations of the world Outside. I was eager to partake of some of the "glamor" I'd been denied in a small Alaskan village.

On the other hand, my folks were very dear to me, and I knew they, especially Mom, would be lonely when I left. I also felt a pang about not graduating with my classmates, and a slight anxiety about adopting a whole new life with a different family and friends. I hoped that I could adapt to a Southern school and that my previous education wouldn't be considered inferior and backwoods there.

Those apprehensions were pushed aside as I said goodbye to my parents and Kenai and Alaska. I didn't begin to realize how brave (some may call it foolish) I really was.

Walter and I flew to Detroit, where with the money we'd received from selling our trailer and a small parcel of land in Kenai, we picked up a new black and white Ford Fairlane convertible and then drove to Savannah, where Walter had grown up. When we arrived, we learned that his family had scattered, and his mother was living in Allendale, South Carolina, with one of his sisters. We moved into her home at the beach for a few weeks, and I enrolled in a Savannah high school. Before long Walter wanted to move to Allendale, too, so I transferred to the school there and we rented rooms from a refined, elderly Southern couple.

Walter got a job delivering Coca Cola to grocery stores, and I finished those last two months of school. I needn't have worried about

Allenale, South Carolina, June 1956

my scholastic standing: my grade point average was the highest in the graduating class. However, because I'd been there such a short time, I was not eligible to be valedictorian. My disappointment was tempered when I received not one but two diplomas at graduation—one from Allendale, South Carolina, and the other from Kenai, Alaska! My high school principal in Kenai, George J. Fabricious, had made sure I "graduated with my classmates." Bless him.

After graduation I took a job clerking in a Winn Dixie grocery store. Valedictorian or not, I have no head for remembering numbers, and in those days before computerized cash registers the job was a nightmare for me. A man who owned a mortuary and also delivered bread to our store offered me a moonlighting job doing cosmetology on his "customers." I was seriously considering giving it a try—we badly needed the money—when I applied for and got a job at the local garment factory.

Because I was young and tall, I was assigned the task of gathering up stacks of folded dusters (ladies' house dresses), carrying them to one end of the factory and stacking them as high as I could onto long tables against the far wall. The women who folded the garments worked on piecework wages and wanted their folding tables cleared as soon as their stacks showed danger of toppling. Consequently, I spent eight hours a day racing like a greyhound from one folding table to another, grabbing piles of dusters and running as fast as I could to the far end of the factory to fling the dusters on the stacks against the wall, where other workers packed them in shipping cartons.

South Carolina summers are miserably hot and humid. The garment factory had no air-conditioning, and by 10 o'clock each morning it was well on the way to becoming a hellhole. By quitting time in the evening, this born-and-raised Alaskan was physically ill from the heat as well as exhaustion and nerves.

God works in mysterious ways. I think He figured I'd been punished enough for whatever sins I'd committed, because after only a few weeks at the garment factory, He got me out of the biggest mistake of my life. And I don't mean that job.

After only 14 months of marriage, Walter announced that he didn't want to be married to me any longer—he'd become involved with another woman. For several months he'd indulged in mysterious disappearances followed by brilliantly creative explanations. He was much more devious than I thought possible. And I was much more naive. Soon after, he handed me a train ticket to Washington, D.C., and $18 in cash and said, "So long, it's been good to know ya," or words to that effect.

As the train chugged north, I sat clutching my Bible and a suitcase, too stunned to do anything but cry and pray. I've always been a pray-er. That day I asked for survival, for the hurt to stop, for my next breath. I asked God to get me through the day. And I got an answer.

I opened my white Bible, the one I'd carried at my wedding, at random, pointed my finger at a verse and read, "And we know that all things work together for good to them that love God." Romans 8:28.

From that time on, I never cried another tear. The hurt began easing, and I was able to draw my next breath. The terrible panic and loneliness lessened. I entered into a rather sad, but peaceful, state of shock. It wasn't an ideal condition, but apparently it was God's way of keeping me sane and getting me through that day and the next few years.

I assessed my situation: I had turned 17 a couple of months earlier, I was a high school graduate, I'd been kicked out by my husband, I was nearly 5,000 miles from home, my ticket read Washington, D.C., I had $18.00 to my name . . . and EVERYTHING WAS GOING TO WORK TOGETHER FOR GOOD!

13

As THE TRAIN NEARED THE CAPITAL city, the porter approached calling "Washington, D.C., Washington, D.C. . . ." I looked out the grimy window and saw a tall, beautiful structure gleaming in the sunlight. I thought it might be the Capitol building, but it turned out to be the Masonic Temple in Alexandria, Virginia. I had a lot to learn.

Union Station in the heart of D.C. was a zoo. People pushed past, hurrying to important meetings and engagements, or so I assumed. The noise was horrendous, the building enormous. I had not the slightest idea what to do or where to go but caught sight of a sign that read "INFORMATION." That seemed a logical place to start.

I approached the woman at the counter and told her my sad situation. Told her exactly as I had assessed it on the train. She seemed surprised at such an outpouring of personal information, but she was sympathetic and helpful. She suggested I get a taxi and go to either the YWCA or the Evangeline, a women's hotel operated by the Salvation Army. I'd heard of the Evangeline in Seattle, and on the strength of that asked the driver to take me there. My first cab ride.

During the trip through the unfamiliar streets of D.C., I again poured out my saga into the ear of the fatherly cabby, who had merely asked what I was doing in D.C. As days went on I often told complete strangers my story, and I've since thought about just why I did that. I wasn't looking for pity or sympathy or a handout. I didn't want to vilify Walter. I think my simple motive was to spew the whole situation out of my soul—to purge myself, so to speak. And without knowing it, I was doing exactly the right thing.

That cabby was a sweetheart. He said he had two daughters about my age and would be just sick if something like that happened to them. He wrote out his name and his wife's name and their phone number on a scrap of paper and told me to call them if I ever got in a real jam. And some people don't believe in angels! I guarded that scrap of paper in my wallet for a year but, thankfully, never had to use it.

At the Evangeline I asked for a room by myself. Most of the rooms were double occupancy, and there was a long waiting list for the few singles. Once again I told my tale, and it just so happened that they did have an empty single, which the kind lady at the desk assigned to me "due to your unusual and unfortunate circumstances."

In the spartan room, I unpacked my suitcase and then sat on the narrow bed, wondering what to do next. I decided to take a walk around my new neighborhood—"L" street between 13th and 14th streets NW—and soon came to a church where a small, almost hidden side door opened into a miniature prayer chapel. On my knees I reminded God that I needed all the help I could get. When I finished there, I felt a lot better.

The next day I sent a telegram to my folks to let them know where I was and ask for a loan of $200. I soon received a wire and the loan, along with my folks' love and support. The loan was paid back as soon as I began receiving paychecks.

Later that day I was eating in the cafeteria dining room when a pretty, petite young woman sat down at my table and introduced herself. She was Wilma Jean Critchfield, from Clarksburg, West Virginia, and she worked in the personnel department of the Bureau of Ships, Department of the Navy. We hit it off like long-lost cousins; soon I found myself telling *her* my life story.

"Well, what are you going to do?" Wilma asked, with real concern in her big brown eyes.

"I don't know, but I need a job—bad."

"Can you type?"

"You bet I can. Mom insisted I learn to type in high school, though I dragged my feet all the way. I'm a good typist!"

As it happens, during those years of the late 1950s various government agencies desperately needed clerks, typists and secretaries. Their personnel departments sent thousands of recruitment letters to high schools, enticing young women to come to D.C. to work for the government.

"You come over to Navy tomorrow," Wilma ordered. "I'll get you an interview."

The next day I bought a map of Washington, D.C., at the corner drugstore and began walking toward the Navy Department. I was thrilled to find the White House directly on the way. I had some difficulty locating the personnel office at Navy, which in those days consisted of many four-story buildings (built some 40 years earlier as "temporary" quarters) across from the Pan Am buildings at 18th Street and Constitution Avenue. At the rear of the Navy complex stretched the beautiful reflecting pool between the Washington Monument and the Lincoln Memorial. Today you'll find the Vietnam Memorial where Navy once stood.

After several dead ends, I located personnel and began filling out the myriad forms required for government employment. An hour or so later, I handed my completed application to a supervisor, aced the typing test and began the personal interview. Things were going swimmingly until a glance at my date of birth brought a soft gasp. "How old are you, anyway?"

"I was 17 a few months ago."

"You look a lot older. Regulations require that one be at least 18 years old to work for the United States government, you know."

I didn't know. "But I really need a job. I'm 5,000 miles from home and have no money. I don't know anybody—"

"I'm sorry." She pushed my small stack of forms back across the desk. "Regulations are regulations, you know."

"But—" and I once again delivered my tale of woe. She was sincerely sympathetic, but sympathy don't buy no edibles. She stood firm on her regulations.

As I was gathering up my forms and purse, a little voice whispered in my ear, "Threaten her." What?! "That's right, threaten her!" Where did that come from? How do I threaten a supervisor for the United States Department of the Navy, for crying out loud?

I turned back to the desk and opened my mouth and these words came out: "OK, here's the way it is. I'm not going to go 'on the streets.' I'm not going to run for home. I'm going to climb to the top of the stairs in front of the U.S. Capitol building, and I'm going to carry a big sign that reads THIS ALASKAN KID IS STARVING TO DEATH BECAUSE EISENHOWER WON'T GIVE HER A JOB. I'll just sit there. And I'll bet I get a lot of newspaper and TV coverage, too."

Her jaw dropped. "Oh, you wouldn't do that—would you?" she exclaimed, her eyes wide. She wasn't any more shocked or surprised than I was. Where on God's green earth had I gotten such a goofy idea? I knew absolutely nothing about politics, and I knew even less about media coverage. I'd never threatened anybody in my life and didn't even know exactly where the Capitol was.

Do you suppose angels recommend *threats*? I believe sometimes they do. I also believe God has a great sense of humor.

"You bet I would," I said grimly as I turned to leave the cubicle.

"Wait a minute, come back here. Sit down and we'll try to work something out." I sat. She stared at me for a minute before rummaging in a drawer for a government telephone book. She flipped pages until she came to a certain agency. On a scrap of paper she wrote the name of the agency, the address, and the name of a person. "Here. You go to this place and tell them your story. Under certain circumstances they'll grant special dispensations. If you get past them, you've got a job here. Good luck!"

I gratefully grabbed the paper and headed out the door before she could change her mind. According to my map, the agency was quite a distance away. I didn't have any money to waste on a cab and didn't know how to use public transportation, so I started hoofing it.

Much later, footsore and weary, I arrived at the address on my piece of paper. After a considerable wait in a stark and dreary reception room, I was granted an interview with the person whose name I'd been given.

Right off the bat he wanted to know why I was such a "special case." Once again I told my story. He thought I'd been dealt a bad hand, too, but didn't think I looked hungry enough, I guess. "I don't think we can help you," he said. Well, it worked once, I'll give it another try, I thought, and brought out my big guns: the threat.

And by golly, it worked again. "Oh, you wouldn't want to embarrass the administration like that, would you? They have enough trouble as it is . . ."

I must have convinced him that I would indeed embarrass Ike and anybody else who stood in the way of my getting a job, because the next thing I knew he handed me a note with the address of the civil service testing facility and told me that if I could pass the civil service test, he would grant me special permission to work for Navy.

Naturally, the testing facility was clear across town, but I hobbled over there—in the high heels we all wore in those days—and passed that little ol' test with ease, despite a pounding backache and blisters on my heels you wouldn't believe. I was on my way! Thank you, Lord.

After that things definitely started looking up. I went to work in Navy's personnel department, right down the hall from my new friend, Wilma. Shortly after, she and I became roommates at the Evangeline.

My job consisted of typing, on a huge, decrepit, manual (that means "not electric" to you youngsters) typewriter. You had to pound those keys like a jackhammer to type through several layers of stationery with carbon papers between. One did not make mistakes, or one had to laboriously erase said mistake on all copies before going on. I typed the same letter all day long. Every day. It was the recruitment letter, personally addressed and sent to young women about to graduate from high school, inviting them to come to Washington and work for Navy.

In no time I could type that letter by rote, and in the process I learned to type with great speed and accuracy. But oh, how sick I became of that miserable letter! After a couple of months I was typing it in my sleep. As my speed and accuracy increased, so did my frustration. The young women I worked with and their older versions, our supervisors, were a nice bunch, but I knew there were better things in store for me than The Letter.

There came a day when word went 'round that one of the engineering groups upstairs, Code 447, was looking for a secretary. I raced up the stairs as fast as my high heels would allow and knocked on the door of Seymore B.'s office. Seymore did the hiring for several engineering codes (groups of some 30 to 40 engineers and draftsmen). Code 447 was one of four codes located in a huge, open room containing around 150 men who sat on tall stools at drafting tables.

Apparently Seymore was satisfied with my qualifications. After a short interview, he dismissed me with: "Tomorrow at 10:00 sharp you come back to see me. But this time, come through the door at the other end of the room and walk down the aisle to my office."

During the months I'd been working on The Letter, I'd been spending my evenings attending modeling classes at Phyllis Bell's Fashion Modeling Agency. Years of movie magazines and Katy Keene comics had given me aspirations of becoming another Suzie Parker. Well, not quite. But I hoped I'd learn some poise, along with fashion

Arlene at work on The Letter

Some of "the boys" at the Department of the Navy

and cosmetic tips, and maybe pick up a few dollars moonlighting as a model. The agency school was about 10 blocks from the Evangeline, but three nights a week I tottered down there after dinner to attend classes on grooming, hair, makeup, walking, sitting, standing, exercises, etc., etc. The lessons were good for me. I learned a lot that had been missing from my Kenai education, and my self-esteem, which had been badly shattered, took a decided turn for the better.

So that morning when I sailed down the endless aisle toward Seymore's office, I was prepared. In a fuzzy, form-fitting, baby-blue sweater, trim black skirt and the inevitable high heels, with my long blond hair brushed to one side and hanging over my right shoulder, I pushed through the heavy doors and launched myself toward Seymore's cubicle.

As the double doors swung shut behind me, 150 masculine heads were raised from blueprints and 300 hands began clapping. Whistles bounced off the ceiling, and feet began stamping on the floor. I tell you, it was awesome. Heart pounding, I determined to give it my best shot. I sashayed down the aisle, throwing kisses right and left and waving like the Queen of England. I've never made a grander entrance nor for a more appreciative audience.

Seymore had been watching through the window in his office, and when at long last I reached him, he stuck out his hand, shook my damp, limp paw and bawled, "You've got the job!"

He went on to explain that most girls applying for jobs in engineering couldn't make it past "the gauntlet." They either burst into tears or ran with flaming cheeks from the room, or both. Since nearly all the guys in the room were incessant teases, Seymore felt he shouldn't hire a girl who couldn't stand the heat. He now knew I could. I think that my years in Alaska in a male-heavy environment went a long way toward getting me through my first day at Code 447, and through the days and months that followed.

I know that today their behavior would be considered blatant sexual harassment. But they didn't mean it as such and I didn't take it that way. They only wanted to see if I had any gumption, and I meant to prove that I did. It was a test—like a typing test.

Once "my boys" learned that I could take any kidding they could dish out, they devised all manner of devilment for my benefit. Once they taped a "Kick Me" sign to my back and I rode all the way home on a crowded trolley wondering why people were snickering at me. Another time they loaded my tote bag with heavy books so when I grabbed it on the run after work, I was stopped in my tracks. A person could have taken offense but I chose to accept their teasing with good humor, and we all enjoyed the exchange. They were the greatest bunch of guys: supportive, complimentary, protective and terrific morale-builders. Despite their high jinks, they made me feel like their princess, and I adored them all.

Joe Breickner, our "Code Head," was a sour-faced, dry-humored bachelor who demanded top-quality work but also allowed me to play grande dame at Code social functions. The six senior engineers were all older fellows—of course, everyone was older to a 17-year-old—who were excellent father substitutes, while the rest of my boys were more of the big-brother variety. After several were gently turned down for dates, they settled for being my friends. One even co-signed for a rather substantial loan for me at the credit union.

My job included typing naval correspondence, some with eight carbon copies, on those antiquated typewriters, and running off copies on an old purple-inked mimeograph. Often I typed reports via the Dictaphone, a contraption resembling a tape-recorder, controlled by a foot pedal. I arranged government transportation when any of my boys traveled, and kept the "spec book" up-to-date as well. Since "'we" were working on the Polaris missile ship anchor windlass, everything was Confidential, Secret or Top Secret, and much written material required shredding at the end of each day. They kept me busy!

During my early days at Navy I took both a civilian secretarial course and a Navy correspondence course, the former in the evenings, the latter squeezed into working hours. With modeling lessons, and an occasional date, it's a good thing I was so young—it was a killer pace. A couple of times I fell dead asleep at the typewriter, giving everybody a big laugh.

When the engineering department had a celebration to wrap up a particular project, several other secretaries and I were asked to be hostesses, serving drinks and hors d'oeuvres and running various games of skill: darts, ring toss, etc. We weren't insulted; in fact, we were pleased to be part of the fun. I never saw any hanky-panky going on at those functions, and I was always treated like a lady. Years later when I heard about sex scandals involving some government secretaries, I was genuinely shocked. I've never believed that sex should be either a toy or a bargaining chip, and if any of the government girls I knew indulged in such behavior, I sure wasn't aware of it.

Although I dated and flirted and had a generally good time in D.C., I managed to maintain my integrity, and I've been glad ever since that I did. Early on I received a letter from a Georgia lawyer saying that Walter was preparing to sue me for divorce, so I felt free to see other fellows. But I was always up-front regarding my marital status. This may not always have been in my best interests, as several dates suggested that since I had "nothing to lose" I might as well enjoy myself. Those guys didn't stand a chance. My Christian beliefs and my fear of the consequences kept my pants up and my skirts down.

Not too long after arriving in town, I walked over to the Capitol one Saturday and took a tour of the building. I wasn't prepared for the beauty and vastness of that great, white monument to democracy, and I spent several hours gaping at the statues, paintings, murals and architectural details.

Entering Statuary Hall, I found a TV crew filming a very distinguished-looking woman. I stopped to rubberneck a while—TV was quite new to me, and it was the first time I'd ever seen filming. Standing behind a barricade of yellow tape, I watched as a bespectacled man wearing a gray suit and a colorful bow tie interviewed the lady.

"What's going on?" I whispered to a young man wearing the navy blazer and name badge of a Capitol page. "Oh, that's Dave Garroway interviewing Senator Margaret Chase Smith of Maine for his TV show," he replied casually. Wow! I'd never heard of either of them, but I was impressed. A TV host AND a senator! It must have been near the end of the interview, for soon the bright lights were shut off, the cameras tilted toward the floor, and the show was over, or so I thought.

As I turned to go, a man wearing a headset stepped over the cables and caught my elbow. "We've got a few seconds to fill up—how would you like to be on TV?" he asked. "What do I have to do?" I gasped. "Just walk slowly around and look at the statues, that's all." And then the director indicated that the commercials were over and we were live again, and the camera swung in my direction. I walked over to the nearest statue of some dead statesman and, craning my neck, gazed with open mouth and glazed eyes at the white marble

At the Evangeline in Washington, D.C.—back row, from left, Judy, Cindy, Bert, Marge; front row, Arlene, Jane, Ruth—on the day of Arlene's "TV debut"

Cindy Jensen

face. Then I leaned forward and peered at the name chiseled on the base. I wrinkled my forehead, pursed my lips and nodded slowly and wisely at the statue—though I still don't know whose likeness I was sharing my TV debut with. Someone yelled, "Cut!" and it was all over.

But that afternoon when I returned to the Evangeline, I was greeted excitedly by a bunch of housemates who had been watching the live show in the TV room. I was famous! I'd appeared with Dave Garroway and Senator Margaret Chase Smith at the U.S. Capitol!

When President Eisenhower won his second term in office, Mom wrote that I absolutely must attend his inauguration. Of course if she'd had her way, I would have attended one or two inaugural balls and sat with Ike and Mamie on the reviewing stand, too. I was still the apolitical youngster: I didn't want to spend a precious day off from work standing with thousands of people on a freezing street corner to see a grinning old bald guy ride by in a convertible. I'd seen Ike a number of times hacking at golf balls on the White House lawn as I walked by on my way to work, and in various parades. This was before the Kennedy assassination, of course, and security was very lax. Oh, for those sweet, innocent days again!

But, wanting to please Mom, I stood sleepily with an Evangeline pal, Cindy Jensen, beside Pennsylvania Avenue, teeth chattering and eyes watering on that inaugural morning in January 1957, and waved and cheered when the president and his lady and Vice President and Mrs. Nixon rode by. I was still four years too young to vote, but I liked Ike and I'm glad I made it to his parade.

Every time a visiting head of state came to town was an excuse for a parade. Government employees were usually given time off and heartily encouraged (read ordered) to congregate on the sidewalk in front of our workplaces, holding small American flags in our hands and cheering lustily for whoever came limo-ing by. I particularly remember Queen Elizabeth II, tiny and prim, and King Saud of Saudi Arabia, who perched his little lame son on the back of the seat beside him as they rode past Navy Department and we waved our flags enthusiastically. The royals probably thought we were cheering for them, whereas we were mostly just tickled to get out of work for an hour. You never knew who might drive by or dart into a government building as you strode the streets of D.C., and it was a thrill for me every time I recognized Somebody.

Sunday mornings I nearly always attended church, usually sampling three or four Protestant houses of worship each month. And for several months after my arrival in D.C., I spent every Saturday and Sunday afternoon either walking around the city or at the old red stone castle that housed the Smithsonian Institute. How I loved the Smithsonian! All that history, those antiques, that junk, crammed into one building—it was like rummaging through Grandma's attic on a rainy day. Now half a dozen huge museum buildings house these priceless treasures.

Some of my favorite exhibits were the First Ladies' Gowns, the Spirit of St. Louis, and Fala (Franklin Roosevelt's dead dog). But best of all was the diorama of taxidermied Alaskan moose, before which I stood each Saturday, miserably homesick.

The National Gallery of Art across the Mall held certain favorites, also. An ebony sculpture of a nude Nubian woman, prone on the map of Africa, her body following the contours of the continent, was so beautifully executed I could hardly keep my hands off it. And for me, Salvador Dali's ethereal Last Supper glows with a delicacy and spirituality that complement perfectly the strength and purity of the artist's draftsmanship.

On those weekend roams around town I dressed like the proper young lady of the '50s: skirts, blouses and high heels. It pains me even now to think of teetering over miles of concrete in heat, humidity and even winter snow atop those three-inch heels. One day I hiked all the way across Memorial Bridge behind the Lincoln Memorial to Arlington Cemetery, but my feet were in such agony I thought they'd have to bury me among the fallen warriors. I sat on a curb, debating whether I had enough money to take a cab back to the Evangeline, and decided that if I wanted to eat until my next paycheck I'd better hoof it back.

The walking excursions weren't only hard on my feet—they were murder on my shoes. But frequently changed cardboard innersoles covered the holes until I could afford a new pair of black pumps, often purchased at the five and dime. The original "cruel shoes"!

It's probably a good thing I did so much walking, as my appetite was never better. The rent at the Evangeline included breakfast and dinner, and I wanted to get my money's worth. For breakfast there were scrambled eggs and hash browns, fruit, toast, and other nutritious offerings, but I was drawn irresistibly to cups of cocoa and several large donuts covered with sugar icing. Dinners featured plenty of fried foods, macaroni, rolls, potatoes, and always cake or pie a la mode for dessert.

Not far from the Evangeline was an eating establishment par excellence: the D.C. Diner, an old railroad car that featured several booths and a long counter and was owned and operated by a jovial fellow named Earl. On Saturdays, Earl offered a hotcake special: all the coffee and hotcakes you could eat for $1.00—and it was free if you ate more than 10. Every Saturday morning after my chores were finished, I'd hie myself over and Earl would serve me my free hotcakes. Such a deal.

It seems strange that with all we were served in the dining room, we were still always scrounging for food. Some of the girls on my floor worked at the State Department and were occasionally recruited to serve as hostesses (a.k.a. hors d'oeuvre passers and hat-check girls) at embassy parties. Sometimes I went along, as it was an occasion to dress up and mingle with some interesting people—but more important, an opportunity to dump a tray of canapes into an oversized purse when nobody was looking. Back at the Evangeline we'd dole the goodies out to our pals as we sat around in our pj's entertaining them with the evening's gossip. Most of us had never tasted caviar or anchovies before but found them quite palatable when washed down with orange soda pop.

You can see why I was having a terrible struggle keeping my weight down. The Phyllis Bell agency expected its models to maintain trim figures, but I was fighting a gaining battle. I did get a few gigs through the agency and a few more freelancing.

I worked the Auto Show and then the Home Show at the Armory, posing fetchingly beside a shiny turquoise Thunderbird or a frost-free refrigerator, and was selected to appear at a Junior Chamber of Commerce luncheon as their "Mystery Girl." A clipping from the Jaycees newspaper is accompanied by a photo of me with an eye mask inked on, a la the Lone Ranger.

Cheesecake-type pictures were popular in the '50s for calendars and postcards and print ads. I suppose nude shots were in demand for

Mystery Girl

Your Mystery Girl luncheon date for March 14th, Phyliss Bell model Miss A. H., was born in Alaska only seventeen years ago. No frigid migid, our blue eyed blond stands 5'7½" tall with statistics looking something like 36"-24"-36½".

Of course, our lovely guest will receive a gift of handsome jewelry from Kay-Franc Jewelers, who have 11 stores here in Washington. We think you ought to come on out to the luncheon and take all of this in.

a certain market, too, but I never got involved with that. I had made up my mind that I'd never pose for a picture I couldn't show my parents or my children. Once I went to a "shoot" and nearly got beaten up when I refused to take my clothes off, but I stuck to my resolve, posed nervously for a few pin-up shots, took the money and ran.

One photographer, whose studio was a long bus ride out in Maryland, took some classical poses of me in Grecian-type draperies and other exotic costumes. We worked in the evenings. His studio was cold and drafty, and the floors were dirty. I have copies of some of the photos, in which my goose-bumps and grubby bare feet are plainly visible. One of the ads for our work:

Go ahead and laugh. I don't blame you. It's embarrassing now, but at least I'm not ashamed of the pictures. I had opportunities to do a lot worse and make a lot more money, but I wasn't *that* hungry!

One such "opportunity" arrived one day as I walked down 14th Street from the Evangeline where a number of sleazy bars and night-clubs as well as a strip joint or two nestled between the neighborhood dry-cleaner and the drug store. That day as I sailed past, the door of one of the strip clubs opened and a large, brassy redhead yelled, "Hey, you, Blondie!" I turned to see what the fuss was about and was amazed to see her marching straight toward me.

"Ya wanna job, honey?" She eyed me up and down through a cloud of cigarette smoke.

"Doing what?" I wanted to know, curious as always.

"Strippin', of course."

"Strippin'? You mean taking my clothes off in front of a bunch of people?" I gaped.

"Yeah. And doin' a little dancin', too."

Well, I was flabbergasted. She caught me so off guard, and she had such *presence,* I was simply knocked speechless.

"But I can't dance," was my lame excuse.

"That's OK, you can earn while you learn," she promised poetically.

By then some of my common sense was returning, and I politely but firmly refused her job offer.

"OK, Blondie," she gave in gracefully, "but if you ever wanna job, you know where to find me."

Several months later I was dining with a date at a local club when I felt a hand on my shoulder. Looking around, I was shocked to see my redheaded "friend" from the strip club. "Hiya, Blondie," she roared. "You ready to come to work for me yet?"

I ran into her several more times on the street, and each time she offered me a "position," but never one I couldn't refuse.

The Phyllis Bell people were concerned about my name. At that time I was Arlene Hotchkiss, a name more suited to a character in a Grand Ole Opry comedy sketch than a model. They suggested I change it to Arlent Kiss—a name more suited to someone who worked for my red-headed strip-club woman! I told them I'd give it some thought and went back to the Evangeline to propose a "Name the Model" contest.

The girls on my floor submitted names for consideration, and the winning suggestion was Lisa. In those days I didn't know a soul named Lisa except the Mona Lisa. I thought it was beautiful, and chose Marie as a middle name, because it's my mother's middle name. Years later, Elvis and Priscilla Presley named their baby Lisa Marie, but I don't think it was in my honor. I was stumped for a last name until I watched a Billy Graham crusade on TV one evening and thought Graham would lend a nice connotation. Amen.

From the Washington Post

14

So I became Lisa Marie Graham. The woman who won the name contest was Sybil, a strapping gal from Great Britain who was a massage therapist and acted in little theater productions. Sybil was six feet tall, built like a Texas cowboy, and spoke the Queen's English as it was meant to be spoken. She also drove a little bitty foreign car, so tiny she could barely fold herself into it, let alone manipulate the gas pedal, clutch and brake.

One November evening, garbed as a Pilgrim, Sybil rushed off to perform in a Thanksgiving pageant. Crossing the 14th Street Bridge, she noticed a flashing red light and pulled over at the "request" of a D.C. policeman. It seems she had a burned-out tail light. I'll always remember Sybil's hilarious description of the face of the policeman as she climbed laboriously from that miniature car, English accent, Pilgrim gown and all.

Now that Wilma Critchfield and I were roommates, we were even better friends. Ostensibly we didn't have much in common: I was 17 and Wilma was 27. I was tall and could pass for 27, while Wilma was petite and looked about 17. I was a divorcee (or well on the way to becoming one) and Wilma was a virgin. She also didn't smoke or drink, the result of a pledge she'd taken as a child at a revival meeting. I was an only child from Alaska, whereas Wilma was a hillbilly from West Virginia and one of nine children. We were Mutt and Jeff, Frick and Frack. And we had more darn fun together.

When I changed my name to Lisa, Wilma decided she'd had enough of her handle, too. She elected to use her middle name, Jean. I can't remember either of us having any trouble remembering to use the new monikers, but I've regretted ever since that I didn't change my name legally. Although I've been called Lisa for more than 40 years, I'm still Arlene on all records and legal documents, and that's been a continual pain in the neck.

My first Christmas in D.C. was pretty bleak. Several girls invited me to go home with them for the holidays, but I preferred being alone. The Evangeline emptied out. The cafeteria was deserted at mealtimes except for me and a few elderly government "girls" who had no families to go to. I was still in shock over the breakup of my marriage, and "I'll Be Home For Christmas," a popular new holiday song, added to my misery. But somehow I knew if I could survive that particular Christmas alone, I'd be able to survive anything. I missed my folks terribly. They sent me a big box of gifts, along with cookies and several fruitcakes, which I promptly devoured single-mouthedly. Not a crumb was left when Jean got back the following week. I went to church on Christmas morning, and took in a movie in the evening. My heart was broken—but sure enough, I survived.

One of my favorite gifts that year was a black velvet baseball jacket with the map of Alaska embroidered on the back and various Alaskan scenes on the front. I loved it! When I wore it, I almost felt as if I were home. Most Saturdays I'd wear that jacket as I clomped about the city taking in the sights. With a straight black skirt and high heels, maybe it wasn't haute couture, but it was definitely comforting.

As Jean and I got to know each other better, she invited me home several times. We'd catch a bus bound for West Virginia right after work, with hard-boiled egg sandwiches and pecan pralines from the bus station, and arrive in Clarksburg late that night. One of her brothers would pick us up and off we'd drive into the hills to the little ramshackle house on cinderblocks that was the Critchfield home.

What a family! Jean's folks reminded me of many Alaskans I'd known: down-to-earth, no frills, hard-working, generous, warm-hearted, God-fearing people. From the older, married kids who had families of their own to Bobbie, Jean's kid brother, they were delightful. I loved them all, and they accepted me as just one more Critchfield.

The whole crew was musical. When the children were younger, they had formed a family band that traveled around the area and performed. Most of the kids, as well as the parents, played instruments, and all of them sang up a storm. When Jean and I came "home" we'd have the best songfests.

When summer came, Jean and I applied for our week's vacation at the same time. I don't know how I figured I'd earned a week's vacation, having worked at Navy less than a year, but I got the time off.

A popular vacation destination for young government workers at the time was Wildwood, New Jersey, a beach community within

The Critchfield family band

Jean Critchfield and Lisa and "the obligatory floppy hats," Wildwood, N.J.

reasonable distance of D.C. We figured it would be closer, cheaper and safer than a week in New York City, and we'd been told it was a great place to lounge on the beach and meet men.

We'd saved enough money for round-trip bus tickets and a week's lodging at a not-quite-beachfront hotel, so with our bathing suits, shorts, a couple of dresses and the obligatory (and very flattering, we thought) floppy hats, we set off with high expectations.

Wildwood lived up to its name. Government girls arrived in droves, while GIs from nearby bases and New York hipsters swarmed in their wake. All you had to do was meet one person who had been there for a day or two, and suddenly you met a whole new crowd.

For several days we had a great time, running around with a bunch of guys from New York. One of them was a big, handsome Italian fellow who had been quite an athlete until he lost a leg in a car accident and was fitted with a wooden prosthesis. He could still dance well, but as the evenings wore on, he'd take the leg off and we'd sit and talk while the others danced. We really had fun with those fellows, but regrettably they had to leave a few days after we arrived.

Shortly before we were to return to Washington, Jean and I went to a club called the High Hat. After the show, which featured a group called the Ritz Brothers, some of the band members invited us to a party at their rented beach house. They had a couple of girlfriends along, and some buddies from New York, one of whom was a policeman, so we accepted the invitation.

Before we left the club, Jean decided for some reason that she'd go back to our hotel instead. I was getting along just fine with the cop, who promised to get me back to the hotel whenever I wanted to leave the party, so the two of us rode with another couple out to the beach house.

I should have had more sense. I usually did. My only excuse is that in the atmosphere of carefree, party-time Wildwood, it wasn't an unusual thing to do. And after all, I was with a *cop,* for crying out loud.

As soon as we entered the kitchen, the other couple vanished. Sitting at the table smoking odd-smelling little cigarettes and drinking what I took to be moonshine were some of the band members. They'd acquired a couple of really tough-looking women—not the girls I'd seen with them at the club. These gals looked and acted like pros. I was decidedly uncomfortable.

My new friend, whom I still thought of as one of New York's finest, must have sensed my dismay, for he gallantly offered to show me the sun porch which faced the beach, thus removing us from the unsavory bunch in the kitchen.

We walked toward the porch down a long hall with several doors on either side. Suddenly this bozo grabbed me and pushed me through one of the doors. I was so surprised I didn't have time to react. He slammed the door, locked it and stuck the key in his pants pocket. Even I knew right away that this was not a good thing.

The room was a musty bedroom. Water-soaked floral wallpaper hung from the walls, and a dirty, torn blind covered the window. The bed had no linen, just a soiled and sagging mattress, upon which I was roughly shoved.

There followed a pitched battle that seemed endless but probably didn't last more than a few minutes. The cop knew some wrestling moves I'd never heard of, and he was strong and mean. I had a blue silk scarf at my throat, which served handily as a garrote. While he was twisting the scarf around my neck, he was busily shedding his pants.

My faith in the power of prayer and my belief in miracles were justified that night. With what little breath I could muster, I cried to God, "Help!"—and God answered. At the last possible second, my attacker passed out cold.

He fell heavily across me, but the grasp on my scarf relaxed, and I was able to wriggle out from under his dead weight. Grabbing his pants from the gritty floor, I searched frantically for the key, found it, and bolted from the room.

Now what was I to do? I didn't have any idea where the beach house was located, except that it was several miles from downtown. My dress was torn half off, and my arms and neck were turning various shades of purple. And then there was that weird group in the kitchen. What could I expect from them?

Another prayer, another miracle. I simply walked into the kitchen and burst into tears. The women had disappeared; the musicians were emptying ashtrays and stacking glasses and Mason jars in the rusty old sink. All four of them turned and stared at the bedraggled girl in the doorway. They took in my torn dress, the bruises, and the tears dripping off my chin.

And to a man, they came and comforted me. "What the (expletive) did that (expletive) do to you?" "Where's that dirty (expletive)?" "Cop or no cop, I'm gonna bust his (expletive) (expletive) for pulling this on a nice girl." I learned at that moment not to judge a person by his appearance.

They led me to a rickety kitchen chair, began fussing with a coffee pot, and before long, we were having very strong, black coffee, and I was blubbering what had happened. Those long-haired, bearded, pre-hippie jazzmen loaned me a pair of jeans and a sweatshirt and when I had changed, told me that my attacker was indeed a policeman but that he had attached himself to their group and was causing them nothing but trouble. They wanted to be rid of him, but apparently he had something on them (maybe the funny little cigarettes). They were increasingly indignant at the way I'd been treated and said they'd drive me back to the hotel as soon as somebody arrived with a car. I ended up fixing eggs and toast for all of us, and we were pals by the time the sun came up and the car arrived.

True to their word, they drove me "home" to a frantic Jean, who was on the verge of calling the cops (!) and reporting me missing. We decided, for the sake of the band, not to report the attack. I hope we did the right thing. I sure didn't want to get those fellows in trouble after they'd been so kind to me.

We'd had all the vacation we could stand. Fortunately it was time to return to D.C., which was starting to beckon like a haven of safety and security. We packed with an eye on the clock, allowing ourselves enough time to walk to the depot to catch the 2:00 bus to Washington. As we hurried out the door, Jean began digging through her purse. "Wait a minute, wait a minute," she howled. "I can't find my ticket!"

Half an hour later we admitted defeat. The ticket was not to be found. She had no ticket, we had no money, this was long before credit cards, and we were due back at work the next morning. We watched from the hotel window as our bus rolled slowly down the street, picking up speed as it headed toward D.C.

The people at the front desk had seen everything and expected catastrophes worse than ours before the long hot summer was over. They were sympathetic, but they didn't have any useful suggestions.

So there we stewed, our luggage at our feet, I with my bruises and swollen throat and Jean wringing her hands and berating herself for her carelessness. At the front door of the hotel stood a man and woman with their suitcases. They couldn't help but hear our troubles. They conferred briefly, then the woman came over and said kindly, "We're driving home to Baltimore. We could give you a lift that far, if it would be any help."

That lovely couple took us to the Wildwood bus depot where I cashed in my ticket and got two one-way tickets from Baltimore to D.C. We rode to Baltimore in real style: A plush new Caddy beats a smelly old Greyhound every time.

You see, sometimes angels come disguised as middle-aged tourists, and sometimes they appear as jive-talking boys in the band.

My folks came out from Alaska for a vacation and were in Washington when I finished my course at the Phyllis Bell Modeling School. Graduation exercises consisted of a gala evening featuring a banquet and fashion show by the graduates, and Mom and Dad were an enthusiastic two-thirds of my cheering section as I received my "diploma" and strutted my stuff on the runway. My other fan on hand that night was a Marine second lieutenant stationed at Quantico who had become a close buddy. Six foot four, and ramrod straight as a gung-ho Marine must be, Gary had an appealing aura of confidence and strength. He was in the same marital circumstance as I, for his wife was also filing for divorce. We were honest with each other and became good friends, though it went no further.

Gary joined me on my "forced marches" around the city, supporting me when my high heels faltered, even half-carrying me up the 897 steps of the Washington Monument.

While Mom and Dad were in D.C., I received papers from Georgia saying Walter was suing me for divorce on the grounds of physical cruelty. Adultery and physical cruelty were the only choices as a legal basis for divorce in Georgia at that time, and since he couldn't use the former, he had to settle for the latter. It was too ridiculous to fight over. Walter had offered to "allow" me to initiate the divorce, but I felt strongly that I wasn't going to be the one to break the marriage vows. Let it be on his conscience if he wanted out.

I could have contested the divorce once he had filed, but by then I knew that I would be much better off without Walter in my life, anyway. Once again, it seemed, "all things were working together for good."

Mom and Dad drove down to Allendale to pack a few household belongings and the rest of my clothes, and I followed by train. When I arrived, Walter and my folks and I drove to Savannah, where we met with his attorney and signed page after page of divorce papers. There was no alimony, no formal dividing of property. We didn't have much to begin with—we'd been making payments on some inexpensive furniture and had made only a few payments on a one-bedroom tract house when Walter decided he wanted to be a free man. We did have the almost-brand-new convertible, but all I wanted were a few of the wedding presents from my relatives, some of the household items I'd saved in my hope chest over the years, and to get back to D.C.

The experience wasn't as bad as I'd feared. I'd already done my grieving, I had no more tears, I was delighted with my new life and loved my job. True, I'd never again be as trusting as I'd once been. And I promised myself never, ever to fall in love and get married again. Never!

When Gary was promoted to first lieutenant, I was at the Quantico ceremony and pinned the shiny bars to his uniform. That was just one of many happy times we had, but somehow he didn't "click" for me. I wanted a big brother/friend, and eventually he wanted something more. We agreed to call it quits.

There followed a variety of nice-enough guys: a Navy frogman with a Joe Palooka nose; a Harvard rich kid who let me help him pick out a Jaguar; another Marine, this time a drill sergeant; a Latin fellow named Fernando . . . But "once burnt, twice cautious." I never dated any of them more than a few times.

One imposssibly hot, humid July day, Jean and I were relaxing in the park near the Evangeline when a man who identified himself as a press photographer asked if he could take our picture for the newspaper. Yeah, sure. However, he had a very impressive camera, and he flashed a press card, so why not? The next day on the front page of the *Washington Post* there appeared a 5 x 7 photo of me in a sailor cap and shorts, feeding a pigeon who's sitting on my wrist. The caption reads: "The soaring mercury didn't faze this cool young lady yesterday. Relaxing in the shade at Franklin Park, Lisa Graham, a Navy Department secretary, fed pigeons and recalled frosty days at her home in Kenai, Alaska." Jean's ankle appears in the lower right-hand corner, partially hidden by another pigeon. Was she insulted! My boys got a large charge out of the photo, and Mom showed it to everybody who came to the Kenai post office.

Does it sound as if the Kid was getting a bit uppity? Don't you believe it. Naive I may have been, and gutsy, and even having some fun—but not conceited. I had my share of humbling experiences that kept my feet firmly planted on solid bedrock. Like the day a floor manager at D.C.'s tony Woodward and Lothrop department store made it humiliatingly clear that the map-of-Alaska jacket and I weren't welcome on the premises. (At least he didn't call me "Blondie.")

The same naivete that got me into an occasional scary situation probably also kept me out of some innocently interesting ones. I usually preferred to err on the side of caution. A couple of nights before the frightening episode at Wildwood, Jean and I were invited out by the comparatively unknown stars of a supper club show we attended. At least *we'd* never heard of Joel Gray and Gary Morton. Besides, I was sure Gary Morton must be married (wrong—Lucille Ball came along later), and Jean thought Joel Gray was too short for her (right). We politely declined.

Ignorance was less than bliss the night my date at a press banquet introduced me to a Pulitzer Prize-winning photographer who instead of shaking my hand gave me a big smack right on the lips. That was probably his standard greeting for female fans, but we didn't do that where I came from, and I wasn't a fan—I'd never even heard of Joe Rosenthal, of Iwo Jima fame. (Remember that in Hope the war had mostly passed us by.) My date thought I should feel honored. That was our last date.

And the day the Phyllis Bell agency sent out a call for extras for a movie being filmed on the Potomac, I made myself scarce. Those Hollywood types were only looking for groupies for their orgies, right? Chalk that one up to Kenai Chapel prohibitions—and don't look for me in any of the crowds around Cary Grant and Sophia Loren in *Houseboat*.

In another category was the evening that several of us girls, including my friend Cindy, were dined if not wined at the apartment of a group of young men from a Middle Eastern embassy. The event had been arranged by a friend of a friend who worked for the State Department, and she vouched for it being on the up-and-up, but it

PHYLLIS BELL'S SCHOOL OF FASHION MOD...

GRADUATES — SPRING 1957

LISA ALLEN
ESTELLE ANDERSON
RUTH ANDERSON
KATHERINE ARNESS
BETTY AUTH
DENA BAIN
BETH BARTLETT
KAY BERKEY
DOLLY BERMAN
HELENA BERMAN
MARGO BILLUPS
MILDRED BOTELER
JACQUELINE BOWEN
KATHLEEN BRIDY
AMELIA ANN BROOKS
BARBARA BROWN
JOYCE COCIMANO
PHYLLIS CALLISTER
ROBERTA CATE
BARBARA CLEMENTS
PAT COYLE
JACQUELINE CRAMBLITT
GILDA DANELLA
JEANIE EUGENIO
NAWAL HELALI FELDER
ROMAN FULLERTON
DEE GAIZBAND
JANET GLASSMAN
DOLLY GOETTLEMANN
JAN GOODIN

HILDA GREEN
MARGARET GROENWOLDT
JANETTE GULA
BILLIE HALE
ALICE HEFLIN
JOHNETTA HEMEY
ELVIE HERBERT
ARLENE HOTCHKISS
HANNAH JEFFERSON
DOROTHY JOHNSON
DITA JONES
ROXIE KELLY
KATHY KERR
PAT KNAPP
MARGUERITE LAFOLLET
NITSA LAKOS
DEBORAH LANE
KATHERINE LANE
CHARLENE LEWIS
VIOLET LITTLEHALES
PAMELA LOUGH
GRACE LUCAS
DOROTHY McCARTY
ROSE MAZZUCO
KATHERINE MASSAS
LAURA M. OLSEN
GAYLE PENNOYER
EDIE PIESTOR
PHYLLIS POOLE
CAROLYN RAMBY

FA
M

I
R
PH
SHI
CARO
ELIZA   OUNG

ctor

tor

Lisa Marie Graham in Washington's Rock Creek Park

has certainly occurred to me since that it could have gone otherwise. They were indeed gentlemen, though, and good cooks, too. We girls focused on the dinner (of course), which included tender, exotically seasoned lamb wrapped in grape leaves, with a flaky dessert so dripping with honey it made your jaws ache. After really thick, really sweet coffee, we accepted the invitation to model some beautiful saris. As I say, it could have gone otherwise. But Cindy and I have only pleasant memories of that evening. She is now Cindy Swanson and lives near Seattle, and we're closer friends today than when we lived across the hall from each other at the Evangeline.

Maybe it was the influence of (non-Pulitzer-winning) press photographers, but I took to wearing a trench coat—my uniform, or my trademark, if you will. Since I still brushed my hair over my right shoulder, I wore a beret on the left side of my head. I considered it a striking costume and was well pleased with my "innovative" look.

The doughnuts and hotcakes were starting to catch up with me, however, and I complained to my boss, Joe Breickner, that my sweet tooth was getting out of hand. He confided that when he was young he too craved sweets, but that cigarettes had taken care of his problem. I went right out and bought a pack of Marlboros—and began a disgusting habit I couldn't kick for many, many years. It did, however, curb my taste for sweets, and helped me keep my weight within reasonable bounds.

So now I could add a cigarette holder to complete my "image." For a time I cringed to recall that very image. But looking at those old pictures now, 40-plus years later, I can smile fondly at the child-woman who needed a flashy facade to cover painful feelings of rejection, and who affected a pose of urbane sophistication to hide her fears. She made it through personal devastation and ensuing culture shock, all on her own. She didn't prostitute herself, literally or figuratively. She didn't become bitter and mean. And she didn't run home to Mama. So what if she looked like a comic book character, or an international spy—or a hooker, for that matter? She survived, and I'm proud of her!

One evening about a year after my arrival in D.C., dressed in my "costume," I was sitting alone in a pizza parlor, mumbling in my root beer and scarfing down a large pizza. I was mourning the loss of

Fernando, who had been transferred to another post, and to further add to my woes I'd decided to stop smoking. It hadn't been a great day.

Through the door came a bunch of girls from the Evangeline. They belonged to a group called the Capital Girls, a quasi-USO club whose main function was to attend dances at the various military installations surrounding D.C. I'd been invited to join their ranks, but the prospect didn't appeal to me, non-dancer that I was. I'm sure they provided a lot of wholesome entertainment for lonely GIs, but I was not even a little tempted to enlist.

Spotting me sitting alone, they crowded into my booth and pestered me to come with them to Fort Belvoir, Virginia, that evening. Their bus was about to leave, and they were on a desperate scouting mission to recruit more girls for the dance. Being in no mood for frivolity, and again, being no dancer, I wasn't interested. They kept at it. I kept shoveling the pizza and turning them down. They insisted, I demurred. Finally the pizza was gone, and my resistance went with it.

Against my better judgment I climbed aboard their bus, accompanied the Capital Girls to Fort Belvoir—and hit pay-dirt. That night I met the man I had been born to love for the rest of my life. That night I met Thomas Stanislaus Augustine.

And that's another story.

Thomas Stanislaus Augustine

Appreciation

MY FERVENT THANKS TO:

Jackie Benson Pels of Hardscratch Press, author of *Unga Island Girl {Ruth's Book}* and my editor, publisher, mentor, and treasured friend. For over half a century we've shared a love of our Alaska homeland, laughed together, and delighted in our own inimitable music. May our stories and our songs endure.

Designer David Johnson, who with style and sensitivity has turned the adventures of a little Alaskan girl into a book we're all proud of.

Werner Pels, computer guru and a very patient, helpful man.

Alma Miller of Hope, Alaska, and Kurtistown, Hawaii, who generously shared photos.

Evelyn Baktuit Boulette, a "Kenai kid" and dear friend who read the manuscript and gave it her stamp of approval.

Charlene and Buck Stewart, who know a lot about Alaska—and spelling.

Peggy Arness and Joanna Hollier in Kenai, Marge Mullen in Soldotna, Pat Williams and Lee Poleske in Seward, and Linda Graham, Ann Miller and Fayrene Sherritt in Hope, for aid in research.

All the friends who read my original manuscript and encouraged me to pursue publication.

My daughters, Stacy Augustine and Michelle Augustine Holmen, of whom I am so proud, and for whom this effort was originally made.

J.T. Holmen for fathering my exceptional grandchildren. I want them to know who their Nana is and how she got that way. Her experiences have helped make them who they are.

Tom Augustine, who for 44 years has given me everything I need —his love. Beyond that, he has supported and encouraged this project in every way imaginable. As we say every night before going to sleep, "I love you, Darling. God bless you."

And ...

My mother, the late Joyce Rheingans Cooper. Some years ago it was my privilege and joy to help her write her memoirs, "Re-Joyce." We laughed and cried over those memories, many of which you'll find in these pages. She was everything a good Christian woman should be, and as a wife and mother she was a tough act to follow. I love her and I miss her.

In addition to "Re-Joyce," my mother's memoirs written for our family, the following books were helpful in writing and researching *The Dragline Kid*:

Bibliography

Alaska Atlas & Gazetteer, DeLorme, Yarmouth, Me. (second ed., 1998).

Alaska's Kenai Peninsula/A Traveler's Guide, text by Andromeda Romano-Lax, photos by Greg Daniels and Bill Sherwonit, Alaska Northwest Books, Portland, Ore. (2001).

Alaska's Kenai Peninsula Death Records and Cemetery Inscriptions, compiled by Kenai Totem Tracers (1983).

"The Ancestors and Descendants of Georg Werner Doring," compiled by Donovan Doring and John Dale (1991).

A Dena'ina Legacy/K'tl'egh'i Sukdi/The Collected Writings of Peter Kalifornsky, Alaska Native Language Center, University of Alaska Fairbanks (1991).

Dictionary of Alaskan English, by Russell Tabbert, The Denali Press, Juneau, Alaska (1991).

Growing Up Native in Alaska, Alexandra J. McClanahan, ed., published by the CIRI Foundation, Anchorage, Alaska (2000).

A History of Mining on the Kenai Peninsula, Alaska, by Mary J. Barry, MJP BARRY, Anchorage, Alaska (revised edition, 1997).

A Larger History of the Kenai Peninsula, edited by Elsa Pedersen, published by Walt and Elsa Pedersen, Sterling, Alaska (second printing, 1988).

Hope, Alaska, centennial pamphlet on Ken Hinchey, edited by Michael S. Kennedy, 1994 (centennial slogan: "There's Always Hope").

The Hope Truckline and 75 Miles of Women, by Dennie D. McCart, Binford & Mort, Portland, Ore. (1983).

Once Upon the Kenai: Stories from the people, compiled by the Kenai Historical Society, edited by Mary Ford, Walsworth Publishing Co., Marceline, Mo. (1985).

Seward, Alaska/A History of the Gateway City, three volumes by Mary J. Barry, MJP BARRY, Anchorage, Alaska (1986, 1993, 1995).

Seward, Alaska/The Sinful Town on Resurrection Bay, by John Paulsteiner (1975).

Swift County, Minnesota/A Collection of Historical Sketches and Family Histories, published by the Swift County Historical Society, Benson, Minn. (1979)

Index

PAGE NUMBERS in bold refer to photographs. People in group photos on pages 116 and 189 are identified in captions only. (Note: Occasionally more than one spelling of a name is found in various "official" and anecdotal sources; an example is the newspaper photo caption on page 12, which misspells Ervin Rheingans' name. In general, where there are discrepancies this book relies on the extensive research in *A History of Mining on the Kenai Peninsula, Alaska*.)

Photo by Werner Pels

LISA AUGUSTINE LIVES WITH her husband of 44 years in the retirement community of Sun City Lincoln Hills near Sacramento, California. Her children and grandchildren reside in other states, so travel is "a joyful necessity," she says, and adventure is always just around the corner. She further notes: "My bra straps are getting longer, my feet are getting bigger, and my hips require more elbow room than they used to. Nevertheless, I'm living happily ever after."

Readers who have made the acquaintance of the Dragline Kid will be glad to know that a second installment of her story—titled *Love, Honor and Oboy!*—is under way.

The Dragline Kid

Project coordinator and editor: Jackie Pels
Design and production: David R. Johnson
Proofreader: Roberta Alexander

Index by A-to-Z WordWright, Seattle, Wash.
CIP data by librarian Rose Schreier Welton
Kenai Peninsula map by David R. Johnson

Rheingans/Augustine family photos, except the Hope community
scenes on pages 66, 116 and 120, courtesy of Alma Miller; the
aerial photograph of 1950s Kenai, pages 132-33, from the estate
of Ralph Soberg (photographer unknown); and the two contempo-
rary views from Kenai on page 155, by Jackie Pels.

Composition by Archetype Typography, Berkeley, Calif.
Printed and bound at Inkworks Press, Berkeley, Calif. INKWORKS

⊕ Alkaline pH recycled paper (Options by Mohawk)

Hardscratch Press
2358 Banbury Place
Walnut Creek, CA 94598-2347
phone/fax 925/935-3422

The Dragline
KID

... Finds adventure in Kenai, Alaska, but hits pay-dirt Outside

$24.00

ISBN 0-9678989-3-5

February 1957